PICASSO'S WOMEN

DATE DUE

Brian McAvera

PICASSO'S WOMEN

Illustrated by Una Walker

OBERON BOOKS
LONDON

e-mail: oberon.books@btinternet.com

A catalogue record for this book is available from the British Library.

ISBN: 1 870259 86 6

1 3 5 7 9 8 6 4 2

A full-length script, incorporating material from three of the monologues, is available from the above agent. This full-length script has been translated into French. Performing rights for the French version are available from Madame Geneviève Ulmann at the Bureau Littéraire, International Marguerite Scialtiel, 14 Rue Chanoinesse, 75004 Paris, France.

Cover illustration: Una Walker

Cover design and typography: Richard Doust

Back cover photograph: Jim Bennett

Printed in Great Britain by MPG Books Limited.

To Una, Rachel and Sarah.
And Michael Quinn

Contents

INTRODUCTION, 9

FERNANDE, 17

EVA, 33

GABY, 61

OLGA, 85

MARIE-THÉRÈSE, 101

DORA, 117

FRANÇOISE, 133

JACQUELINE, 163

Acknowledgements

I would like to acknowledge a small grant from the Arts Council of N. Ireland; also the help of Alan Drury, Jeremy Mortimer, and especially the director Michael Quinn.

INTRODUCTION

Picasso's Women: an overview

There were numerous women in Picasso's life, but eight of them were central. Art history and biography have dealt with them harshly, and in my view with grotesque unfairness. They have been represented as dumb, venial, mental, vicious – indeed there is scarcely a pejorative adjective that has not been applied to them. Most of this stream of abuse has been from the hands of men: but by no means all of it.

Picasso's Women is a series of eight monologues for actresses. Ideally they would be performed consecutively, in chronological order, though each is free-standing. However the notion of a series of overlapping perspectives – like a cubist painting or sculpture – makes more dramatic sense.

Each monologue lasts roughly twenty-five to thirty minutes. Each is in a different style, suited to the individual, and to the artistic period of Picasso that characterised the relationship.

As Dora Maar, perhaps Picasso's most intelligent mistress, pointed out, there were five factors which influenced his way of life and his style. They were:

1. The woman with whom he was in love at the time.
2. The poet or poets who acted as catalysts.
3. The place where he lived.
4. The circle of friends who provided admiration, and understanding, and admiration, and more admiration...
5. His dog.

Usually, when wife or mistress changed, so did everything else.

Therefore, each of the monologues reflects the period of art that Picasso was working on (Blue to Rose period for Fernande with Max Jacob as the central poet. Main period 1904 – 1909, and so on). But these monologues are from the women's viewpoints, not Picasso's. And stylistically they reflect this.

Dora Maar was a photographer for example, and a highly intelligent exponent of surrealism. She also suffered a nervous breakdown (most likely driven to it by Picasso). Therefore the form and imagery of Dora's monologue is much more radical than that of, say, Marie-Thérèse Walter who was a sensuous, easy-going, relaxed woman whose intellectual equipment was somewhat limited.

To place the women in perspective, the following is a brief account, in chronological order, of the major relationships that Picasso had with women.

1. Fernande Olivier (main period: 1904 – 1909)

Fernande spent many of her early years in Paris with Picasso. These covered the periods which art historians have called the end of the *Blue* period, as well as the whole of the *Rose* period, (so-called because of the dominant tonalities of his work during these years), and the beginning of the *Cubist* period. She was a – if not *the* – crucial element in the bohemian existence of the early Picasso. Max Jacob was the crucial poet of the period along with Apollinaire.

She was the only woman in Picasso's life who seemed to show no real bitterness towards him, even though she was unceremoniously dumped when he began to 'make it'. Generally treated as a rather dumb sensual woman by historians, she was certainly sensual – and anything but dumb. Her first husband, whom she married at the age of seventeen, went insane six months later.

Picasso kept her like an odalisque in a harem – he even did the shopping and housekeeping so that she would have no excuse to leave the studio. She was the model for all of the women in the 1906 painting *The Harem* which was itself a kind of 'dry run' for *Les Demoiselles D'Avignon*, perhaps the artist's most famous painting. It is my contention that this latter painting is actually a venomous attack upon Fernande.

It is often argued that Fernande must have been stupid with respect to art as her memoirs fail to mention Picasso's most famous and momentous painting. But this is to see life through the lens of an art historian: a fatal problem for both art historians and biographers who rely upon them. We now know that Fernande kept a diary; that she actually left Picasso during the period that he was working on *Les Demoiselles D'Avignon* – a turbulent and traumatic period in her life – and, as I speculate in the play, that she had a fairly explosive sexual reason for not wishing to discuss the work and all that it meant for her.

2. Eva Gouel (main period: 1910 – 1915)

Unceremoniously dumping Fernande, Picasso lured Eva away from her husband, a minor painter called Louis Marcoussis, and eloped to Spain with her. When they returned, it was to a more bourgeois existence, having moved from Montmartre to Montparnasse. A petite bourgeoise who wanted stability and security, she undoubtedly brought order to Picasso's life, and his paintings became a rich mixture of sensuality and sadism. But she suffered from ill-health: within two years she was dead from tuberculosis.

She was the only woman whom Picasso refused to discuss with a later mistress (Françoise Gilot), and he secretly kept paintings of her until his death. As her health worsened, the international scene grew more ominous – with World War One in the offing.

He never painted her in any recognisable form: as Douglas Cooper pointed out, it was as if she was his, to be hidden away and savoured. Apollinaire is the crucial poet, cubism the major artistic phase. His paintings of the period contain multiple concealed allusions to her.

3. Gaby Lespinasse (1915 – 1917)

No one seems to have known about her at the time. It wasn't until Douglas Cooper, the art historian, revealed her existence in the late 1980s that it was realised that she was one of the 'Picasso women'.

Picasso proposed marriage to her – the first time he did such a thing – but she refused!

She was a friend of Eva's, and was twenty-seven when she met the artist, who was then thirty-three. Within two months of Eva's death she was intimate with him. But she was also married, to a Mr Lespinasse who had a love-nest at Saint Tropez which, it is said, she used without her husband's knowledge.

Perhaps fearful of being controlled like the other women in Picasso's life, she opted for a free and easy life in the company of Lespinasse and his friends who, it is also said, were always only too ready to sacrifice work for pleasure. She was the first really independent woman that he met – and she broke him, at least temporarily.

4. Olga (main period: 1917 – 1927)

'A woman who could pursue only one idea at a time, with the utmost tenacity' according to Pablo, Olga was the daughter of a colonel in the Imperial Russian Army, and a minor ballet dancer in Diaghilev's company. She provided Picasso with children, a tight rein of domesticity, and an entrée into Society which gave him a level of social stability, stature and security so far unknown to him. They moved into an elegant quarter, full of antique dealers and the like, and lived an opulent life.

She has been characterised as rigid, obsessive and possessive – indeed tyrannical. But compared to her predecessors she was a sexual innocent.

Art history has treated her savagely, reducing her to the level of a caricatured bitch, determined to wreak vengeance. But in reality she was a conventional, socially ambitious and sexually repressed woman, accustomed to order and social entertainment, who was forced into a combustible relationship with a man who was fascinated by her as an exotic specimen, but had no intention of ever giving her what she needed – a loving and permanent relationship. There are good grounds for believing that her later behaviour was the result of some kind of psychotic episode, most probably caused by living with Picasso.

Neoclassicism is the art-period and Cocteau the reigning poet.

5. Marie-Thérèse (main period: 1927 – 1936)

Marie-Thérèse was, in legal terms, an under-age seventeen-year-old schoolgirl when Picasso accosted her at a metro station. She became his mistress and, so far as we know, never had sex with anyone else. She was a gymnast, a physical fitness fanatic, and she possessed a remarkably voluptuous body which appears in every conceivable form in Picasso's work. She was virtually unknown to Picasso's friends for the first fifteen years of their relationship.

Critics have not dealt kindly with her, considering her as dumb, stupid, ignorant – simply a body. She was undoubtedly beautiful. She was also faithful – and in many ways she gave the painter more than anyone else did, either before or since.

However, there is little evidence that Marie-Thérèse was dumb, or stupid. She wasn't an intellectual but she was honest, truthful and emotionally perceptive. She was also kind, generous, thoughtful and entirely unmoved by the razzamatazz surrounding Picasso.

Fernande, Olga and Marie-Thérèse are classic demonstrations of the art industry's inability to deal with women – especially women who are perceived to be in a role as wives, mistresses or models – as *people*. Characterisation is reduced to caricatural shorthand. If a woman is not overtly conversant with the critic's frame-of-reference, then she is ignorant of 'Art'. If she fails to discuss particular highlights of the artist's life, then she is unaware, insensitive or imperceptive.

It never seems to occur to such critics to discuss Picasso in such a light. Nor does it seem to occur to them that there are different kinds of intelligence; different kinds of emotional sensitivities. They rarely task themselves with the notion that these women might have a myriad of reasons for not wishing to discuss certain things. And to a man – and often to a woman – they refuse to look at the emotional, psychological and socially-determined freightage of events which together had such a decisive impact upon the lives of these women and others like them.

6. Dora (1936 – 1945)

Once Marie-Thérèse had provided him with a daughter, Picasso went window-shopping. The poet Éluard introduced him to the bluestocking, painter, photographer and member of the surrealist circle – Dora Maar. Picasso was fascinated when he saw her in a cafe, performing the feat of sticking a sharp knife in between her fingers, at speed, into a table.

She always represented the 'weeping woman' to him, being – as male critics would have it – highly labile and subject to frequent emotional crises. By 1946 she had been briefly hospitalised, having become psychotic, and was then treated as an outpatient by the psychoanalyst Jacques Lacan.

Dora was a formidable artist – and artist-photographer, in her own right. She is only now beginning to get due recognition, especially for her early work. As ever the art industry reduced her to the caricatured level of a Picasso groupie. Her emotional instability was ruthlessly exploited by the painter who was only too happy to have other women competing for his affections and who had no qualms about having her committed, and subjected to electric-shock treatment.

Her personality changed, as they say, overnight. Her work changed just as radically: for the worse in my opinion. I have little doubt as to where the blame should be laid.

7. Françoise (1945 – 1953)

When he was sixty-two, the painter saw the twenty-two-year-old Françoise, sitting at a table in a cafe, and rushed up to her with a bowl of cherries. He had been disgusted at Dora's breakdown which he saw, typically, as a sign of inexcusable weakness that held the sign of death for him.

It was a stormy relationship as she rebelled against his paternal dictates, and their relationship was punctuated by bouts of work-paralysis on Picasso's part. She finally did what Picasso had considered unthinkable – she left him!

She was the only woman to do so, publicly. She has spent her remaining life establishing herself as a painter.

7. Jacqueline (1953 – 1973)

A divorcée at twenty-five, and a relative of the family who owned the ceramics factory at Vallauris which Picasso made famous, Jacqueline 'took over' Picasso's life. I must look after him. Art critics argue that the painter surrendered to her, living out the rest of his life as the prize of a woman who tyrannized him through idolatry. When he died she kept a vigil beside the corpse until it began to decompose.

She also isolated him during life, to such an extent that none of his children could even see him. One son committed suicide when not allowed even to attend his funeral. Jacqueline herself blew her brains out, shortly after Picasso died.

~

Picasso, who claimed that women were either goddesses or doormats, was and is the most revered artist of the century. He was also a total bastard, using people and discarding them like spent condoms. He could be charming, fascinating, generous, even kind; but he could be ruthless, calculating, meanminded, manipulative and vicious.

He attracted devotion, and women. He immortalised them on canvas and in his sculpture – and he broke most of them on a rack which was partially of their own making. The crucial influence in his life was probably his mother, whom he left at the age of fifteen.

At the end of his long life, Picasso was still frantically painting the pleasures of the flesh. The Tate Gallery produced an exhibition of this late work and the catalogue, together with legions of later art critics, has tried to persuade us that these works are a summation of a Master Artist's life. In a way they are: they are a testament to a man who regarded women as stimuli for artworks, as occasions of sexual exploration, but rarely as individuals in their own right. The women have had the last laugh: it is the laugh of those who watch him spasm in a reflex of the wrist upon canvas, endlessly turning out repetitions of himself.

Brian McAvera, 1999

The first four monologues from *Picasso's Women* were broadcast on BBC Radio 3 between the 13th and 17th May 1996, directed by Michael Quinn. The roles were played as follows:

FERNANDE, Hannah Gordon
OLGA, Barbara Flynn
MARIE-THÉRÈSE, Josette Simon
DORA, Lindsay Duncan

FERNANDE

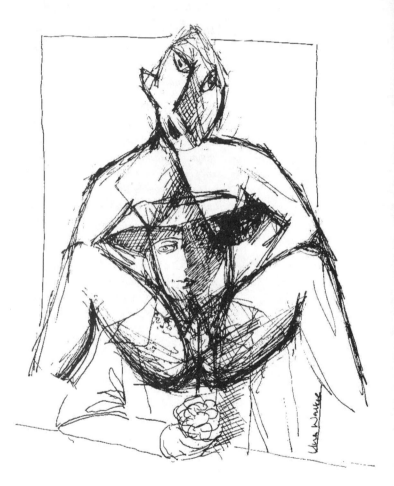

Fernande, it is said, had a beautiful voice. Everyone remarked that she spoke an impeccable French, very correct, very stylish, albeit with a lacing of the Montmartrois argot. Likewise, it is said, she gained a diploma which enabled her to teach at primary level, though whether she ever did so, seems doubtful.

She did, however, teach French to foreigners and, when times were hard, also gave classes in deportment to well-bred but impecunious young ladies. The memoir which she wrote of her time with Picasso is notable for its lack of cant, its lack of bile, and its elegant limpidity.

Art historians like John Richardson casually note her promiscuity – which was rather limited – without caring to use the same word of Picasso, a rampant user, and abuser, of all things sexual. Said historians call her writing 'amateur' while yet grudgingly admitting that she gives unrivalled pen portraits. They call her accuracy into question, ignoring that she was writing a memoir (and was thus not too concerned with the specifics of dates), and conveniently ignoring that almost every other 'historian' of the period is positively cavalier in terms of dates, places, incidents and the like. It's hard to escape the conclusion that many of them don't like women that much.

Fernande was not the dumb, ill-read, visually illiterate individual that many would have us believe. She was much better read than Picasso for a start! But then again, this is my construction of Fernande, so let her speak for herself.

~

Chopin's Polonaise in A minor *drifts in, and lingers. A shaft of light illuminates FERNANDE. She is playing Patience, seated at a small card table, absorbed in the game. The flick of the cards is the only other sound.*

FERNANDE: Ten on the nine... five on the six... seven on
the seven, four on the four...
(*The Polonaise builds towards a climax, then ebbs. She looks up.*)
(*Plangently.*) Are you listening Pablo?
No... I don't suppose you are. (*A beat.*) It's strange, isn't it
Pablo, that the cool eternity of death levels us all:
The artist and his model...
The artist and his mistress... The artist and his... ego!

(*Limpidly.*) I was happy to die.
Eight years I had, with you; another two before
Apollinaire, Braque and Derain were fighting in

the trenches; another four before the war had ended and poor Apollinaire, trepanned, was dead of influenza, just two days before the armistice... You were careless of your friends Pablo... you scattered them like confetti to the winds of your imagination.
(*A momentary edge of acidity.*) Useful.
Useless. Deceased while alive.

(*Nostalgic warmth gliding in.*) Eight years I had with you Pablo, before the long trek to mediocrity. Eight years, Pablo, the happiest of my life... better than what had gone before... better than what was to come after...
... eight years...
I offered them freely, you took: I have no cause for quarrel... (*Simply.*) ... you are what you were...

(*In elegiac mood.*) And now, you too are dead, lurking somewhere in this echoing limbo, aware of your four score and ten but a prisoner of what you always were... *but only had left...* when the breath slipped out of your recumbent body.

(*Amused at the ironies.*) Your wrist exercised itself with pencil or brush, slipping into vagina, sucking on nipple, caressing the curve of a naked body, no longer able to translate the act to the art.
(*Almost admiringly.*) You were dead long before you died Pablo!... but like a dog caught in the act, you just kept on going. You always kept on going. A dogged energy.

(*Teasingly.*) Oh... I'm not one to moralise Pablo... I've led a far from exemplary life, especially in my youth... but fifty-four years of grinding mediocrity is a handsome penance, especially when one is aware of...
(*An edge of emotion: the core of her being is naked.*)
... having been touched by... (*Almost reverently.*) ... genius.

(*Surprised at her younger self.*) I never did tell you about myself, did I Pablo? You accepted me as you found me,

in the Bateau Lavoir, married as you thought to that sculptor manqué Laurent Debienne...
(*A smile in her voice.*) Laurent, the eternal student...

I had run away, one franc fifteen in my pocket, was hungrily staring at the window of a *pâtisserie*, when an arm slid under mine, guiding me to a table, and this bearded young man was buying me coffee and croissants.
Could Laurent, the sculptor, do a portrait of me?
(*Elated.*) Me! (*A beat.*) That night I slept in his studio. The following morning he arrives from his home with bedding, cologne, and curling tongs!
(*Businesslike.*) I became a model.
From 8.30 to 12.30. For a sculptor like Carlier or Sicard. My clothes covered in plaster. Five francs.
1.30 to 5.30. For a painter like Carolus Duran, Boldini or MacEwan. Cold. Tired muscles. Five francs.
And after dinner, a few hours for Laurent. No francs.
(*Making a point.*) To pose well you have to forget that you are posing.
Before long I was posing for the famous!
Henner had met me when MacEwan was ill. 'A model? Good. Take off your hat, your corsage. *Bien ça va!*'

(*With a quickening of excitement, and pride.*) Then it was the magisterial Corman, at work on enormous historical canvases. Many were the famous, and influential, political personages who posed for him, with me... made eyes at me, made offers...
(*Tartly.*) One learns to accept a compliment, and no more, gracefully.
(*A beat.*) One looks, poses, listens to artists talking, discussing, striving, notices the long hours, the discipline; one begins to draw, to sketch, to paint, to realize what a real artist is...
(*Dryly.*) To realise that this is not a category which contains Laurent.

(*Gaily.*) The younger painters like Dufy or Friesz would take me round the galleries. Even when I was a little girl, my uncle would take me to the Louvre, and admire the naked flesh of a Bougereau. 'So realistic!'

(*A beat.*) When I was a bigger girl, well used to the naked flesh of posing, I entered the Luxembourg and saw, with a sudden and startling clarity, the new worlds of Renoir, Degas, Toulouse-Lautrec; Monet, Seurat, my beloved Manet; Van Gogh, Guillerman and especially Cézanne.

(*Opening of The Sorcerer's Apprentice by Dukas.*)
Who am I Pablo? What made me? What clash of ignorant armies did battle before I was delivered, mewling, to an uncertain world?

Born out of wedlock to Clara Lang.

(*Softly, plangently.*) *Who* were you maman? Why did you never come?

For me...

Mon père?... (*Hesitantly.*) ... papa... Monsieur Belvallé.

(*Seeking warmth.*) He would come to see me some two or three times a year. I remember a tall, remote man in a top hat who would hold me by the hand, bringing me into a shop to buy a rubber doll. He had warm, thick hands, gloved in soft and scented leather. I could have hidden in those hands.

(*A beat.*) His half sister raised me. They liked *their* daughter.

No caresses for me...

(*Controlling her sense of loss.*) I always used to say that my mother had died in giving birth.

(*Accepting it.*) Perhaps, in a way, she did.

(*The quiet unsettling opening of Ravel's La Valse before the orchestra enters.*)
When I was fifteen, I started a diary, a journal... a page to talk to.

Almost three years later I met *him*, small, black eyes,
Paul Émile Percheron: shop-assistant.
Shops were nice. My daddy brought me into shops.
And Paul was nice. He held my hand. He stroked my
face. He bought me trinkets. Then he took me to a hotel,
took off my clothes... and he rammed it into me, and
when I screamed he slapped my face and punched my
shoulders and again he rammed it in and pumped it up,
and down, and up, and down, like a wheezy plunger in a
blocked drain.
(*Holding back an edge of tears.*) No caresses for me...

(*Deadpan.*) When she found I was pregnant, Madame
gave me a choice. Marry him, or else the reformatory.
Fine choice.
So I married him.
He would lock me up, often take away my shoes. 'Get
rid of it', he said. Then. 'Open your legs'.

(*A beat.*) There were five steps outside the door. It had
iced over, then snowed. I remember floating into the air,
turning over, and then my belly bumping down, down,
down to the ground. He needn't have worried.
(*With a slow and bitter irony.*) Didn't I get rid of it?

It was a few months later that I ran away, with one franc
thirty to spend a future.
Who am I? *Not* Percheron, *not* Lang!
(*Brightly.*) I remembered the bible classes: the Mount of
Olives. Did not the dove bring an olive leaf to Noah to
show that the flood had subsided? Was not the olive
grove sacred to Pallas Athene, a symbol of peace and...
(*Almost afraid to say it.*) ... fecundity?...
... and so I became an olive grove... Fernande (*With
pride.*) Olivier!

When Laurent and I found a home in the Bateau Lavoir,
I gave *him* a new name: Gaston de la Baume –

the Gascony Lad of the Healing Balm! He soothed away
the bruises... !
New christenings... new beginnings...

(*Opening of Chausson's Poème.*)
It was such a strange building, the Bateau Lavoir.
On the peak of Montmartre Hill, the top floor opened
onto the Place Ravignan, the floor that you and
I, Pablo, would soon use... but all of the other floors
could only be reached through a different entrance,
nearly twenty metres below in the Rue Garreau. Like
the huge barges used by the washerwomen, said your
friend, Pablo; and my friend, the poet Max Jacob; and
the nickname stuck.

Laurent was a nice man... but I was... was... frigid.
Sometimes I let him... he didn't ask for much... most
times, over the years, I didn't. Then one day this
excitable Spaniard followed me in the street, right back
to the studio. It was strange.
(*Animated.*) You can pose, naked, or clothed, in front of
old artists, young artists, good artists, indifferent artists
but they want their work more than they want your
body... it's safe.
I didn't like *him*, Joaquim, one of your friends as it
transpired, but I loved his body. It was the first time that
flesh *excited me.* Spare, hard, tight muscle.
A bottom you could cast in plaster and caress for ever.
Touchable, strokable... physical... responsive...
(*A half laugh.*) My life before you, Pablo...

(*Teasingly.*) I used to see this 'other' Spaniard, Pablo,
forever chatting with his friends under the chestnut trees
in the Place Ravignan.
Whenever does he work?
(*Enjoying herself.*) There was nothing particularly
attractive about him at first sight, just those eyes, that
expression, looking at you, the odd half smile, the lock
of hair brushed across the forehead, the blue boilersuit,

the uneasy, awkward, disturbing presence. His hair was
shiny, black, obstinate.

I'd be at the water tap, just past the front door,
filling up a bucket, and there he'd be, chatting away,
watching.

(*Rumble of thunder. Clash of lightning. Sudden driving rain. We
hear wind and rain through the following, recessed...*)
(*With longing.*) August the fourth, 1904.

The first time he spoke to me.
There I was, sitting under the chestnut tree, enjoying the
late afternoon sun, reading, when – thunderstorm! I was
racing into the doorway, soaked already, when there he
was, waiting on me, standing on the stairway, a kitten in
his arms.
Then it was in mine!

(*With quiet amusement.*) He spoke execrable French,
halting, heavily accented. I wanted to teach him.
He just laughed.
Big heavy eyes. Pensive. Full of contained fire.
We went to his studio. Your studio. (*A beat.*) There was
a rusty cast-iron stove topped with a yellow earthenware
bowl which was his hand basin. To the left a deal table
with a towel and butt end of soap. In the drawer, a white
mouse. To the right, a tiny black trunk which, along with
a rush-bottomed chair, was the seating arrangement
for guests!
There were no curtains but the windows were painted
blue. On the floor were the artillery of brushes in bottles,
tins of oil, a bowl for nitric acid, tubes of paint, the
empty ones squeezed and tossed in a corner, and easels
sashaying on the drunken floorboards. Between the
boards the thick cracks had filled and overspilled with
dust, tacked down with flecks of paint.
No dusting! Would stick to the canvases!

There were rickety easels, an oil-lamp...
problem solved... he only painted by night!... there were
canvases, huge blue unfinished canvases, stacked
everywhere.

(*A beat.*) He was working on an etching. A wretched,
emaciated couple, sitting at a table with their frugal
meal. Her breasts sag. They are looking away from each
other but his long etiolated fingers are a tender comfort
to her shoulder and her arm.
This man, this painter Picasso, *knew*! He could
register pain and poverty, silence and solace, tenderness
and resignation, sadness... and oh so sensitively...
compassion...

We made love on the mattress in the corner alcove.
I forgot Émile. I forgot Laurent. I forgot Joaquim.
He burned away their images in his steely blue world, as
if inside me, his brush was recreating another me,
making me live calmly, strongly, vibrantly, drawing my
canvas in the rose of my flesh, opening my body to the
flush of ripening paint.

(*The wind freshens.*)
(*A beat. Without malice.*) And what I didn't know, my
poor, thin Madeleine whom I never met, though you
lived close by, was that as I made love you, who were
pregnant, were at his behest, having... an abortion.
(*Wind tails off into a dull drizzle.*)

(*With pride.*) I wouldn't move in with you Pablo. You
kept cajoling me. Kostro, you'd plead, looking at
Apollinaire, what to do?
Kostro – he was like a six foot pear with an
emperor's nose and books tumbling out of his
capacious pockets – would discourse on an eighteenth
century text, which he'd give me to read, discuss
the footnotes in an edition of the Marquis de Sade,

noting that as a small Spaniard, Pablo was ill-equipped
in certain directions –
(*Amused.*) Pablo did *not* like being teased –
– then he'd read the first draft of a poem he'd scribbled
on the back of an envelope as he walked to the studio,
before rounding off by comparing the plastic qualities of
Pablo's latest to the real thing – me!
But what to do?!, mutters poor Pablo, so Max is rolling
his trousers to display his short hairy legs, each hair a
character in a play that he will act out.
'She loves you'. 'She loves you not' 'She'll cut off
your –'
Max, dear Max, biting, sarcastic, gloriously vulgar;
Kostro and he, like big child, small child, taking baby
for a walk. Kostro writing notices of Pablo's work,
Max scuttling down to the second-hand dealer Père
Soulier with a sheaf of Pablo's drawings: ten centimes
a drawing, three francs a gouache – cash!

(*A Chopin chord – Polonaise in A minor.*)
(*Unsentimentally.*) Days long ago when the world was
ripe, dream days, golden days, before my hair that you
cusped had bleached the years; before my hands that you
kissed had wrinkled and soured; before my laugh that
you loved had dried in the throat.

(*Briskly.*) Eight years later, when they arrested Kostro,
because of stolen statues that you had bought, you
denied him, like Peter while the cock crowed.
Nearly thirty years later, as Max was being taken to a
concentration camp, you refused to use your contacts.
(*A beat.*) He died there.

(*With regret.*) Oh... you took and you took and you took
Pablo, but your only gift was the promise of an eternal
life... in a painting.

(*High-speed clatter of footsteps, racing down wooden stairs. She is up and
looking round as if Picasso is bounding down the stairs towards her.*)

27

September the third, 1905, five o'clock in the afternoon.
I summoned you:
'I have decided to move in with you Pablo. You
understand that I expect to be treated as a lady'. ¿*Lo
entiendo*?
With one bound you were lugging my trunk, and then
I was in your alcove where, above the mattress, you had
made an oratory: a packing case draped with the white
lawn blouse that I had worn, the day you took me from
the storm.
There were two blue vases, Louis-Philippe, filled with
imitation flowers... (*A long beat.*) ... My papa had made
silk flowers, and artificial plants...
(*Driving back into it.*) Hanging from a nail on the wall,
mounted with the material from a worn-out blue chemise
that I'd left in the studio, was a sketch, shaded and
shaped and sensuous, of me... me!
Lady Madonna, with a crimson rose, in silk, underneath.

I was to stop posing. So I did.
If a man eyed me in the street you might shout or
scream or produce your pistol.
Often you would take away my shoes, and then do
the shopping.
If I was propositioned, (*Amused.*) a regular occurrence in
Montmartre, you would lose your temper and accuse me of
conducting an affair. So, instead, I became your odalisque,
sleeping, reading, hidden away.
It was irksome.

(*With verve.*) But on Tuesday nights we would walk across
Paris, Max, Kostro, André Salmon, Pablo and me to the
rowdy 'literary' soirées at the Closerie des Lilas where
Gauguin's friend, Jean 'I'm a Baudelaire only with more
colour' Moréas would needle Pablo, flamboyantly yelling
'Has Velásquez any talent?!!'
Pablo *liked* Velásquez...

He was introduced to opium there. He bought an opium

pipe with a long bamboo which had an ivory tip, a little
oil-lamp, and a box of the oily paste.
Everything suddenly seemed clear and bright and good,
until one morning, myself and Pablo found a young
German painter who smoked with us – he had a bald
head – hanging in the window of his studio.
Some people blamed Pablo for his death.
We stopped smoking.

But I anticipate, don't I Pablo? I coloured your canvas
with madder and rose. If we sold work, then it was
off to the Cirque Medrano, and you were painting
saltimbanques and tumblers and acrobats, me amongst
them... (*A long beat.*) ... playing with a child.
You dedicated that to me.
For Kostro it was Harlequin, alone, in adoration of a
child. And then there was Gussie Van Dongen, two years
old, who would waddle in to play calling 'Tablo! Tablo!
Fedande! Tablo!'
(*An edge of anguish.*) But a child wouldn't come, for us,
would it Pablo... you painted a whole world of prepubescent
boys, and girls, with breasts tipped with red, like cherries...

I was frightened of you sometimes. Once, someone rushed
into the studios, shouting: 'Frédé's shot a thief !'
Many's a time had we scoffed a meal on tick at his cafe
where the walls were decorated with works by indigent
artists like Utrillo, or Pablo!
I ran down to the cafe where a crowd had gathered.
You were there. You saw me. You walked over to me.
Then, suddenly, your huge hand was colliding with
my face – like a shot from your pistol – and the crowd
gaped, fell silent. And you dragged me back to my
comfortable cell...

Well, Pablo, men should weep, women are sheep: way of
the world; no cause for complaint. I am what I was.
(*A brisk chord.*)

We all knew that you *would* be famous.
From ten in the night to six in the morning: sacred
to work.
Dealers slid in and out. Max publicised. Kostro
publicised.
Then Leo and Gertrude Stein appeared, having bought a
painting from Sagot. We went to the Steins' salon and
there was a Picasso, hanging beside the Cézannes, the
Matisse, the Manet! Vollard started to buy! Cleared out
the studio. Twenty paintings! Two thousand francs.
Enough to live on for three whole years!!

(*Debussy's Iberia.*)
So we went to Barcelona, your mama, your papa, your
gaggle of admiring friends, with myself the picture of
Parisian elegance in a new dress and a fine hat and a waft
of Parisian perfume, *Essence de Chypre*, and I posed, oh
how many times I posed, for their photographs.
Didn't they all want to photograph me!
I saw the looks, the nudges and Pablo, didn't you seem
to grow and grow and grin, for wasn't I a prize possession,
and wasn't I proud to be the prize of such a promising
painter!

Such a rich and promising painter!!
Then to Gosol, high in the Pyrénées, inaccessible except
by mule!
He shaved his head on arrival...
Enchanted land, simple land, a pure pure air.
A ruined medieval village at the slope of a mountain
with at its feet the modern village. A smuggler's land,
borderland, simple people who brought us partridges and
thrushes to vary the bean and sausage stew. *Cocido*!
You kept painting me, naked, opening me, closing me,
like the slices of an orange.
I was your harem, Pablo. That's what you called the
painting: *The Harem.*
You painted me, four times, the one canvas, combing my

hair, drying myself, raising my arms, looking in a mirror,
four times, naked times. Me. Opening. Out. For you.

(*Hard, driving.*) That was the acorn Pablo, but look what
you made of the oak.
That was, that... brothel painting... *Les Demoiselles
D'Avignon.*
You tore me apart, Pablo, dislocated me, cut me, made
me a whore five times over, made me fetish, crude,
brutal, disgusting...
... but I didn't tell, did I Pablo?
Nothing in my diary Pablo...

(*All passion spent.*) We were back in Paris. I knew you
wanted a child.
So I went to the nuns.
Raymonde was her name, scarcely fourteen, so pretty. We
all loved her. Such tenderness you showed. You sketched
her again and again.
I had gone on an errand, came back early.
It was happening again, as with Laurent.
I had gone to model but the artist was sick. When I came
back, there was a thirteen year old girl, naked, in
Laurent's bed.
She was modelling for him, he said.

(*Controlling herself.*) I took Raymonde back to the
orphanage.
Pablo kept working, in a frenzy, on his brothel painting.
Hard, angular, geometrical, penetrating.
(*A beat.*) We decided to part.
I moved into an apartment, not far away. Miss Stein
arranged for me to give French lessons, to her friend
Alice.
They paid for the flat.

(*A chord, plangent...*)
Maybe I misunderstood... you kept coming to see me.

Eventually I went back.

Money and fame came rolling in. We moved to a smart apartment, a rollercoaster of fine objects, important people, beautiful women. I even introduced you to Eva. You became distant.

I tried to make you jealous: a young Italian painter. I moved out, eleven francs in my pocket. Within a day you had left with Eva for Céret.

I followed. You and Eva left.

I never saw you again.

(*Deadpan.*) For a while I worked with Poiret, the couturier. He went bankrupt.

Then I was an assistant at an antiques shop. It closed down.

I recited poems in the *Lapin à Gill*, was a cashier in a butcher's shop, then cast horoscopes.

One has to survive.

(*Without bitterness.*) Apartment 42, Rue du Bois de Boulogne. Four metres by three. One room.

On my card table I play Patience.

A few souvenirs, arthritis, old photographs.

No caresses for me.

When I died they found the little heart-shaped mirror that you'd bought me as a present.

I kept it safe Pablo, I kept it safe.

How many of us are there, Pablo, companions of artists in their youth, in good times and bad, growing old, alone, with only their memories as constant companions. Didn't you tell me once: 'To be forgotten is worse than to be dead'.

(*A beat.*) What if you're both, Pablo?

(*As she returns to playing Patience, Chopin's <u>Polonaise in A minor</u> drifts in, rises to a climax, then fades as the lights fade to blackness. Under it we hear her voice. 'Ten on the nine... five on the six...' etc.*)

The End.

EVA

Teneste la Promessa (entering at 'O come son mutata...') from Act III of Verdi's La Traviata is playing as she glides onto the stage, a slender ethereal figure in a Japanese kimono. Her head crooks, like a delicate bird, as if she has heard something from the dim and distant past. For a moment her eyes glaze before she summons up the courage to face her past, and present a face, for us, in the present.

The music fades. She coughs.

EVA: Pablo had a horror of illness, disease... Should you catch a cold, you were trying to kill him! And if he once suspected that I was diseased... had an *infectious* disease... one that spread on the breeze of a cough or a sneeze... then I knew that he would leave me... Mycobacterium tuberculosis. Not hereditary... but infectious, or so it seemed... at the start... Could affect all parts of the body: the bones and joints; the lymph nodes –
(*With a touch of humour.*) Scrofula!; the abdomen; the meninges and the central nervous system; and the skin – lupus vulgaris!
But the cleverest tubercule, the consumptive tubercule, was like a little seed that grew and grew, a mildewed garden of the lungs, spreading, decaying, disseminating, putrefying.

Who was I?
I was in love!
What if I had some vague chest pains, was listless, my pulse unsteady?
What if, every now and then, it was a night sweat, a running nose?
What if my flushed face at night became coldly pallid in the morning light?
What if a hissing of the chest would rack me suddenly into a foul sputum in the white of my handkerchief?
(*She coughs.*)

(*With light humour.*) I changed to red handkerchiefs.
My make-up was as elaborate as a Japanese geisha.

I was very, very careful.
Pablo had a horror of illness...
He would talk to some doctor.
See image after image.
Bacillus after bacillus, knocking on the doors of the lung.
How the tissues of the lung shake hands with the uninvited
guests, then ambush them, engulfing them with protective
cells. How these cells grow into tubercules, then swell and
swell and swell until they slough off into the cavernous
rooms of the lungs.
Then, as the bacillus disintegrates, a toxin is produced...
tuberlin... poisoning the bloodstream.
And as the body slowly putrefies, it spits out more and
more of its little seeds... little flotillas seeking a host to
birth a death.
Pablo always knew where to get advice... the best
of advice...
Not hereditary, but infectious; or so it seemed at
the start...

*A rope swing descends from the Gods as the <u>Libiamo</u> chorus from La
Traviata plays. The ropes are bedecked with an elegant arrangement
of painted flowers and foliage, and the seat is a vibrant sea-green.*

I was calling myself Marcelle Humbert.
It helps to have a husband, should you be in need of one.
I wasn't, but one never knows.
I was a 'charming young lady'. That's what they said.
That's what I ensured that they said.
Charmingly unpredictable.
If one is going to live and have a reasonable standard of
life, and needless to say if one does not wish to have to
work for a living, then one needs to find an agreeable
companion; one who is capable of acquiring the necessary
finance.

Not that one should be idle.
If finance is provided, it is one's job to be thrifty.

To run the household with precision. To decorate
and make a home.

To be on the lookout for a better class of companion...

(*Sitting on the swing.*) My first intelligent choice was
Louis Marcous, a Pole, whom Apollinaire later
Frenchified into Marcoussis. He was an older man, in his
mid thirties, when I met him. A friend of Max Jacob's.
Slim, slender, protective.
Used to talk about his home city of Cracow: the Mariacki
church with its Veit Stoss altar; the medieval market-place
thronging with Russian traders; the artists' cafes and the
theatres... the puppet-theatre...
He had only been in Paris for three years when I met
him but he spoke perfect French.
Cultured. Took me to Chopin concerts. To the opera.

Of course he was an artist.
Had been painting like the Impressionists but I soon put
a stop to all that.
A decline in the family fortunes meant that he had to
earn a living.
Didn't he do the occasional *dessin humoristique* for *Le
Rire*, *La Vie Parisienne*, and *L'Assiette au beurre*?
If I was going to live with him, he was going to have
to stop spending most of his time painting, and do a
proper job.
Didn't they pay well for cartoons?

Of course they did. Especially *his* cartoons.
In no time at all we were moving to a better apartment
on the rue Delambre, buying Dufagal furniture; a decent
dinner service.
He kept hankering after painting though.
In his later years, or so they tell me, he used to ask
every critic, every collector, whether he would be
forgotten. Had he not spent most of his life trying

to add his little stone to the imposing edifice of the History of Art?

Poor Louis. He missed the point.
What does it matter if you're dead?
And if you're alive, then the only thing that matters, assuming that you have something to sell, is your eye for investment and appreciation.
Poor Louis: he had nothing to sell – apart from his cartoons.

Now Pablo: that was a different matter! He had collectors already.
About the same age as Louis.
Perfectly positioned for a woman with an eye to investment and appreciation.

And what an eye he had! It could strip you at forty paces across a crowded room.
His basilisk eye I used to call it!
You might be sitting at the far end of *La Rotonde*, daintily perched on a wicker chair, but you could still feel the heat of his glance.
You knew what he was thinking, could almost see the hand glide over the sketchbook as he lipped a rounded nipple, curved into the bosom, then licked along a thigh.
You knew that this man had no interest in a quick tumble and fumble and thrust against a wall in an alley. No, he wanted time and flesh and his tongue pressed deep inside you. He wanted you wide and full, eager and grasping, then clasping your legs to his flesh like the pin of a broach. He wanted you yelling, screeching, your breath sobbing in great gulders of pain. He wanted you biting and scratching, scoring your lust across his back... like a scraper on an etching plate.

And that, of course, was part of the appeal...

And that – of course – was the final problem.
He never wanted *you*.
You were just the means to a fuck on the whiteness of
the sheet.
And after it was over, he would dissect his reactions...
would dissect you...
like an object... like a surgeon dissecting a cadaver...
and he would translate the results of his enquiries onto
page or canvas.

(*Music: Parade of the Tin Soldiers by Leon Jessell [CDA 66998.
Hyperion]. Run underneath.*)
Louis and I were doing nicely, thank you very much, even
if he did harp on and on and on – in a quiet gentlemanly
fashion – about wanting to return to 'the necessity' of
painting.

We would entertain visiting Poles, hold dinners for writers
like Francis Carco or Pierre MacOrlan.
Louis was very fond of writers. He even read their books;
wrote reviews in the newspapers.
Sometimes we would go to the Cirque Medrano. Once
we met Braque there.
Louis liked Braque who offered to introduce him to
Picasso and so, one evening, we walked down the
Boulevard Rochechouart to the *Cafe l'Hermitage*
which, as I soon found out, was just down the road
from Pablo's studio.

It was cheerful and friendly with a very loud orchestra
and, as Louis said, full of pimps that had strayed in from
one of Francis Carco's novels. There were the strange
futurists who wore a different coloured sock on each foot;
writers and critics like Salmon, Jacob with his Jewish wit
and the pear-shaped Apollinaire; painters like Braque and
Derain, built like boxers but quiet as puppies; and dealers
like the shrewd Kahnweiler. Small, immaculately dressed
and with perfect manners. They called him The Little

Japanese on the Butte. Wives, mistresses, models from
the Pigalle, boxers, actors, anyone who was anybody
in Montmartre.

*Segue into intro of Charles Trenet's <u>Menil Montant</u> from Le Fou
Chantant [EMI France 790 6312] with just a touch of the lyric.
She walks towards us, to the left of the stage, sits at a cafe table and
pours herself a glass of wine. Besides the carafe of wine, there is a
French newspaper, a packet of cigarettes and a box of matches.*

He was sitting with Fernande, smoking a pipe.
He wasn't saying much but he was the centre of attention.
There was a lock of blue-black hair that had a life of
its own, sweeping down over his broad forehead,
obscuring an eye so that Louis quipped that he looked
like a handsome Cyclops.
His shoulders were broad and he had long arms, like
a monkey's, only thicker, and with long slender fingers,
that drummed restlessly on the table if he were being
bored.
You had to entertain him, as if it were his right to be king,
and yours to be court-jester. He sat legs apart, short legs,
but powerful thighs, waiting to bestow the benediction of a
fuck on whomsoever he considered worth a few minutes
of his time.

She was watching over him jealously, eyes ceaselessly
roving to ward off competition. Before we had even
threaded our way to the table, I knew I could take him.
Knew that I would have to play the game.
This man would not like scenes.
We sat down, myself beside Fernande, and I could see
him evaluate.
Fernande was big and buxom, a Rubens – as Max would
later say – to my Watteau.

It was time to make friends with Fernande.
Time to get her talking and agree with her.

Didn't I look like Evelyn Nesbit whom Fernande adored!
I did!
Wasn't Evelyn a former chorus girl and model!
Why thank you kindly... I am slim... and supple, ain't I?
Hadn't her oh so rich husband, Harry Thaw, murdered
the architect Stanford White, and all because of her!
Really?
What it must be, to be so in love with someone, that you
would murder *because* of them!
True love!

We took to going out, the four of us.
First to the Cirque Medrano, then to a cafe.
Sometimes we would visit: dinner at the Steins'.
Gertrude – I called her Miss Stein at first but she insisted
– Gertrude liked me. She was built to last, like a railway
carriage, and she had money.
There was a Picasso on the wall.
Louis was so ashamed at being considered a cartoonist
when all around there were paintings by Cézanne and
Matisse, Picasso and Derain.. and Braque.
Silly man: he was making good money as a cartoonist!
And then, when I left him, he threw it all away and
started to paint like a cubist!
Silly, silly man...

Fernande liked me.
She thought that I was no threat.
Told me of Pablo's moods and sulks, how cruel he could
be, how roving was his eye.
All the little things she had to do to please him!
It was time to take Pablo in hand. To plan...
She would take a lover, enjoy herself for a while and then,
when the time was right, she would run off for a few days,
run off with this young and handsome body, a body with a
nice pert bottom, slender shoulders and strong mobile
hands...
It would make Pablo jealous.

Naturally.

Pablo took another studio, one in the Bateau Lavoir, well away from Fernande's eye.

Naturally!
The way to a man's heart is through his loins so we fucked there, frequently.
It was no hardship.
Fernande, I could tell, was not an active lover.
Had perhaps a limited horizon when it came to the out-of-the-ordinary.
I enjoyed... the unusual.
And I know he did.
I was punctilious and precise. And inventive. And knowledgeable...
He wanted me, more and more and more.

It was just a matter of timing, and of organisation.

(*Germont's Di Provenza il mar, il suol, from La Traviata, fades in.*)
Then Fernande came across a young Italian painter, Ubaldo Oppi.
Handsome but penniless.
Could I be a go-between?
(*We hear Giordani's Caro Hio Ben [Cecilia Bartoli. Decca 436 267-2 DH] run under.*)
Well...?
Didn't I know what Picasso could be like, how insanely jealous he could become...
True...
Best not give him the opportunity to find out...
No...
Not just yet!
(*Fade out Verdi.*)

I used to take her letters to the Italian and his to her.
How grateful he was.

How trusting she was.
Didn't she tell me that once read, she used to tear them up
immediately and drop them into the toilet, for safety's sake.
Just at the point when she decided the time was right –
for a quick two-day elopement – and she had made the
arrangements in writing...
I brought the letter to Pablo!

Just like a man.
I even had to tell him what to do.
I would deliver the letter to Oppi, and his reply to
Fernande. She would throw it down the toilet and run off
with Oppi.
But before she did, Pablo would confront her with the
evidence of her deception, claiming that he had found
the evidence clinging to the sides of the toilet! He would
break it off with her, and then, the next day, Pablo would
run off with me!
For Pablo, things always had to be someone else's fault...

And so it was!
Poor Fernande!
Such a silly woman in matters of finance.
Weren't we both on the look out for a husband? And yet,
after six years or more, she had failed to present him with
a child.
Stupid.
I did not intend to make the same mistake. A few years
to make oneself indispensable, and then, *l'enfant*!
Pablo was Spanish. Give him a son and you would have
the title Wife, for life...

Stupid too, Fernande, when it came to the art of making
money.

If you have an artist who is acquiring collectors and
dealers, who has a *reputation*, then it behoves one to flatter
such people, to organise carefully selected soirées with
exactly the right dinner guests and exactly the right menus.

One imparts information judiciously.
So-and-so is also after such and such a picture.
And by the by, did you know that Pablo had just exhibited
in the Armory show in New York, at Der Sturm in Berlin, at
Sonderbund in Cologne... at the Grafton in London?

Miss Stein had not been buying lately.
Pablo and I were fucking merrily in the Bateau Lavoir.
He always worked especially well if he was... content...
I needed to show him that I would be an asset as well as
an available body.
So I said to him. She has called round once or twice,
hasn't she?
She left her calling card.
Why don't you flatter her sense of her own importance.
Paint her calling card into one of your compositions.
So he did.
And she bought!
And I knew that I could help to make this man into a
figure of financial substance!
And I did!

(*Fade in Moonlight on the Alster, Track 14 by Oscar Fetrás [Hyperion
CDA 66998.] Run under.*)
He never painted me, did Pablo. Never even drew me.
Not a proper painting like those he did of Fernande or
Olga or Jacqueline.
Not even a proper drawing like those of almost every
casual slut whose legs he opened, for inspection with
his pencil.
Only me, the ghost in the machine of his art... only me...
unmemorialised, unrecorded, unmade into art...

Oh, they'll tell you otherwise.
How great the fiction for the myth of the mighty man!
There is a painting, found in his studio after his death,
called *The Artist and his Model*. Painted at Avignon
in 1914.
I should know.

I was beginning to die. I knew. He knew.

He knew I was too weak for a roll in the bed.
He was not a man who went without.
Nearby were the brothels.
Max knew all about them! Didn't he spread the story that
Les Demoiselles D'Avignon were the young ladies in the
famous establishment of that town?

So, what was I saying? Ah... *The Artist and his Model.*
It makes a fine story – poor Pablo, so much in love,
paints a picture of me, the only picture of me, done in a
manner of some realism. He hides it away in his studio,
a secret icon to venerate until the day he dies.
Oh such love, such sentiment.
Is he not, underneath that carapace of iron, a sweet and
sensitive soul?

What matter that there is a tiny problem with this
touching story!
A tiny problem of truth.
She is an attractive lady, this neoclassic model, posed in
a 'studio', uncovering her pudenda, unaware of the man
who watches her.
But she is not me!
Look at my photographs! Does she have my ears, my
cheekbones, my eyes, my mouth, my figure?
Of course not!
They will tell you that this 'masterpiece' is an idealised
image of me.
Stuff and nonsense.
It is a young lady from the brothel in Avignon, displaying
her wares for the customer.
(*Fade out.*)

Even when I was almost dead, he did two drawings: *Eva
Dying* and *Eva on her Deathbed.*
I remember, having died, I took a last look at the artefacts

of this man, in relation to me. There I was, stretched out on the bed, like a corpse that has been cut up and re-assembled.

No face, no presence, no trace of emotion, no after-image of the woman who had shared his bed for five long years. Even in death, he turned me into an exercise in style and vision, exorcising out my image, exorcising any 'love' he may once have had, editing that which was me – out...

I know what you think.

You think. Silly cow. She deserves it.

Didn't she scheme behind the broad back of Fernande?

Didn't she spread the word that Pablo had offered Fernande to Louis in part-exchange for me?

That Germaine Pichot had given the pox to half of Montmartre?

Didn't I say that it was a waste of space for a woman to destroy the reputations of her enemies: she should start with her friends?

So what if I did?

Didn't Pablo scheme behind the back of every woman with whom he ever lived?

Didn't he lie and cheat and try to destroy the life of poor Juan Gris, just because Juan wouldn't abase himself in front of the Master?

Didn't he ruin the lives of his children?

But he lives to a ripe old age and I am struck down in my prime.

Is it fair?

A bird in a gilded cage – ideally with a mechanical chirping bird – is slowly lowered from the Gods, to shoulder height, stage right, to the accompaniment of Le Printemps from Verdi's Les Vêpres siciliennes [Sony SK 52 489 000]. She glides over to it, rests her finger for a moment against the bars of the cage, then smiles to herself.

Poor Fernande.

Off she went with her Italian. Cut off by Pablo without a sou.

Off we went to Céret.

Pablo was taking no risks.

He throws out Fernande on the evening of May 18, 1912.
On the morning of May 19, we leave in such a rush that
he is busily writing letters from Céret.

There was the dog, of course. A huge half-Afghan that
used to take him for walkies.

Dear Braque, Please make arrangements for sending on
Frika.

Not to mention bedding.

Dear Kahnweiler, please send bolsters, sheets, blankets,
my linen, my nice yellow kimono, the one with the
flowers...

But of course!

Dear Braque, Please get Madame Pichot to look after the
monkey and the cats.

But more importantly –

Dear Kahnweiler, Please make a package of canvases
and panels from Rue Ravignan. Any canvases sketched
with charcoal should be fixed first by Juan Gris. Please
send the palette – wrap it in newspaper first – and tubes
of ivory, white, emerald green, Verona green, Peruvian
ochre... I need them at my side...

Braque writes back. Dear Picasso, Just met Ramón
Pichot. The family are coming out to Céret for the
summer and they're bringing Fernande with them!

Pablo panics!

Why is he being hounded by this woman? It is most
unreasonable.

We try Avignon.

Pablo reckons we should be where no one will think
of looking for us, so in the suburbs, out past the
railway viaduct, the factory chimneys, the billboards
and the sheds we find, in an avenue of plane trees, the
Villa des Clochettes.

Squat, imposing and ugly.

Just like Gertrude!

And empty.
Just like Gertrude: hungering to fill the void.
Pablo whitewashes the walls so that he can sketch.
It is stiflingly hot but this seems not to bother Pablo.
Sudden rain storm, the roof leaks, and we sleep under
an umbrella!

I am enjoying my Pablo and he is enjoying me.
Braque comes to stay nearby with his wife Marcelle so
I, Marcelle Humbert but born Eve Gouel, become
hispanicised to Eva.
It is as if he has two wives, this Spaniard in the works,
one for work and one for play.

The wife for work makes of him an intellectual child:
paper, sand, stencils, pieces of mirror; cinders, sawdust,
grit; fabric, coffee grains, bits of newspaper, bottle labels;
wrapping paper, imitation marble or wood, the contents
of a wastepaper basket... arranged and re-arranged on the
sheet, connected by charcoal lines or a crisp brushstroke,
and tweaked with a kind of visual pun by the use of
house-decorator's combs to simulate certain kinds
of surface.

Marcelle Braque was not pleased.
She had me for company and wasn't she a friend
of Fernande's?
Wasn't her recent husband spending most of his time
closeted with the superstitious Spaniard?
Weren't they even cooking together, making a soup of
powdered almonds, grapes, garlic and bread!

Oh they stimulated each other. And I stimulated Pablo –
constantly.
He was like a dog on heat, pricking his penis, scorching
his semen in a blaze of ideas.
A perfect triangle.

From which Marcelle was exempt.

I stoked him up like the temperature in August.
Didn't risk wearing anything but big shorts, did he?
Too much evidence!

Collage, *papiers collés*, paper sculpture. This was the
apogee of cubism and I made it happen. *Nature Morte à
la chaise cannée...* Still Life with Chair Caning.
The first collage, sexed into life shortly before we
came here.
I told him. Even the intelligent artists and collectors are
having difficulty in following your work. It's so abstract,
so divorced from life.

If you want to be difficult, fine! If you want to be
complex, fine! But give people some clues... like a
crossword puzzle... and then they will think that they
are even cleverer than the artist!
Put things together, don't take them apart!
Didn't Kahnweiler keep on insisting that the public
needed help?
Look at Braque. Those bits of lettering that he's doing.
Why don't you take it a bit further? Stick in some bits
of real life!
So he did!
And when it came to the cut-out paper sculpture, well...
who was it did embroidery? Not Pablo?
Who was it cut out patterns and made her own clothes?
Clearly not Pablo!
Who was it suggested dressmaker's pins so that he could
try out different options when pinning bits to a canvas?
Who else?

(*Fade in Philip Houghton's* Stélé *performed by John Williams
[SK 60586]. Fourth movement. Track 19.*)
You know that sculpture, the one of the guitar with the
sound hole made out of a cardboard tube?
Who do you think showed him how to make it fit?

D'you think a man would have that dexterity?

Oh he knew what I was worth... He made a painting
specially for me, of a guitar, decorated with the words
'I love Eva'; and a gingerbread heart.
Hadn't he bought me one, not six months past, at a fair
on the Boulevard de Clichy?
(*A beat.*)
And when I died, the gingerbread heart disappeared...
(*Fade out.*)

He never painted me. Never even drew me. Not once
does my likeness sketch the legend of our relationship.
Oh he memorialised me. In graffiti. Like a schoolboy
carving initials on a tree; like a dog, peeing against
the bark.
At the start it was like a game between us. He would
write 'ma jolie' on a painting so that Fernande
wouldn't find out about me. Then he had his little
marks, his ciphers, such as the sign for my pubic hair,
and the words 'I love Eva', seemingly lost in the
immensities of a cubist nude.
You would need a magnifying glass and a route-map to
find it!
Then, when we were a couple, he wrote the words in a
big childish script.
For a man who was so precise with a drawn line on a
page, he had no finesse when it came to handwriting. An
impatient scrawl.

He was impatient about most things, was Pablo.

(*Fade in Alfredo and Violetta's Parigi, o cara, noi lasce remo from
La Traviata.*)
I told him that we should go to the theatre, the ballet. He
would enjoy the sets, the music, the beautiful actresses!
Sarah Bernhardt was playing in *La Dame aux Camélias* in
Avignon. Violetta, the heroine, a courtesan who is dying

of consumption, is told by her lover's father that, unless
she renounces him, she will ruin, not only his life, but that
of his sister as well. She makes the supreme sacrifice.
And Bernhardt was magnificent.
Theatrical, artificial, but magical.
She was in her sixties yet she made you believe in
her passion.
Pablo sat and grinned his way through the performance.
The sets? Pah!
The music? Pah!
Sarah Bernhardt?
*She mimics the tragic gesture of one arm over the eyes, the other
arm extended.*
Pah!
He could be very dense at times, my Pablo...
(*Fade out.*)

Of course he wasn't mine.
I used to think that my soul, my essence, was in his
works.
Some distillation of all that was me; a secret liqueur which
only the cognoscenti could scent.
Silly.
Just like Fernande...

I suggested that he move out of the studio in the Bateau
Lavoir. Why give him the opportunity for another liaison?
That was Fernande's mistake...
Kahnweiler put up a 'For Rent' sign.
We moved into a fine, but gloomy, new studio apartment
on Boulevard Raspail.
Soon contracts would be up for renewal. Find out how
much Derain and Braque are going to get before you
renegotiate, I said.
He did.
Kahnweiler agreed to buy a minimum of twenty drawings
a year as well as all the paintings and the gouaches.
Drawings at one hundred francs each.

Gouaches at two hundred francs each.
Paintings at between two hundred and fifty and three
thousand francs each, depending on size.
Pablo was very prolific...

Naturally I furnished the apartment in some style. But
I was always careful with money. Provided accounts
for every sou.
Montparnasse was so much superior to Montmartre. A
better class of person. A better class of cafe. One could
foregather of an evening in *Le Dôme* or *La Rotonde.*
Professional people. Respectable artists.
I was... happy. And I provided an impeccable service. Ten
fifteen a.m. Slip out of bed and bring back coffee for two.
Wake Pablo. We would sit in our matching pink-and-white
striped pyjamas.
Perhaps he would want a cuddle, or maybe something a
little more strenuous?
Service provided.
Now, is the following agreeable for lunch?
Service provided.
It was always... agreeable.

Pablo would go to the studio and I would service
the apartment.
Washing. Cleaning. Ironing. Plumping the cushions.
Tying back my silk-brocade curtains. Polishing
the furniture.
Changing the bed linen: as crisp and white as one of his
primed and stretched canvases.
Lunch. Perhaps a spot of shopping while Pablo worked on.
Making lists of potential collectors. Finding out about
their taste in food and wine.
It was an agreeable life.

Summer came around and this time we stayed in Céret.
As you walked on the mountains, you crushed lavender,
rosemary and thyme.

Max, who came with us, grumbled about the pederasts and the ether-drinkers in the local cafes but Max would grumble about anything.

We were staying in a converted monastery, with orchards ripe with fruit trees and crumbling brick walls – so beautiful that each morning, as we woke to sun streaming through the tall high windows, we would feel at peace with the world, make love, and Pablo would reek of painterly energy and I would giggle with Max, go off with him, and Manolo and Frank de Havilland, both of whom lived in that glorious building, and we would 'do the sights'.

Braque and Juan Gris arrived, and such was the sense of a summer's spoils, looted from the earthy Gods, that Pablo would even cease work and all of us would career across the Pyrénées to a bullfight, into the land of squares and angles where Max claimed that the people were as bitter as their aloes.

Then Pablo's father died, and it rained... and rained... and rained. I had only rope-soled shoes.

Pains in the chest. Angina? Bronchitis?

And I started to cough. Sore throat.

And after the funeral, Pablo cannot find it in himself to work.

While he was away I went back to Paris and saw my doctor. Maybe I was pregnant!

But no. He sent me to a specialist.

Cancer. In the early stages. Not to worry. Treatment, when caught so early, was often successful. Chemicals, in the form of soothing ointments and salves.

A tonic of potassium arsenate.

If I knew then what I know now!

If only!

Drink the tonic and it causes cancer of the lung...

What is a cancer?

A cancer is the growth, unchecked, of abnormal cells.

Purposeless. Preying on the host. Almost indestructible.
Like Pablo.
I was coughing more and more. I knew I had to tell him
before he feared the worst – tuberculosis.

Strange. He was so... kind.

At summer's end we were back to Paris and another new
apartment.
Pablo consulted Gertrude who sent us to Doctor Rousseau,
123 Boulevard Montparnasse. Eight months later, I had the
operation. Enough time to recuperate before we went for
the summer to Avignon.
But I knew: no chance of marriage now...

5 bis, Rue Schoelcher.
(*Laughs out loud.*) My last resting-place, so to speak.
Not gloomy like 242, and only a minute's walk away.
A huge atelier window, like the prow of a ship, scanning
over the cemetery of Montparnasse, and right beside us,
built by an important Austrian architect, this imposing
Jugendstil edifice!
It was quiet. A better class of people. And on the second
floor! Bliss!
There were soirées chez Serge Ferat and his 'sister', the
Baroness D'Oettingen, where one would meet proper
writers like Apollinaire, Salmon, and Blaise Cendrars;
and well-behaved painters like De Chirico, Derain,
Severini and Survage.

Pablo decided to learn Russian. For the duration of
the winter.
Pablo. Learning Russian.
Pablo who couldn't even master grammatical French
after ten years in Paris!
But I'm sure the Baroness was an inspired teacher.
Didn't she take Apollinaire to a hotel for an entire
week once?

Didn't poor pear-shaped Ap tell me that it was the
happiest period in his entire life?
So nice to have a gifted teacher, don't you think?

I tired easily. But my armchair, fringed and upholstered,
was wonderfully comfortable.
To sink into its padded and luxurious resilience was a
comforting solace from the pain.
Pablo would sketch, before he left for a lesson and the
small hours.
Woman in an Armchair. Lots of sketches. Finally a painting.

Oh you can find me if you look hard enough.
His thoughts were elsewhere so I became an interesting
excuse for compositional enterprise.
How do you commingle the European and the world of
Tribal Art?
Why, cut a woman in half of course: one half of each!
How do you commingle sadism and sensuality?
Why, toss in a few crossword clues of lingerie – scalloped
silk and garter – then mix with long pointed breasts,
nailed to the torso with tent pegs.
Torso.
Ciphers for body parts.
A stained smear of wiped blood.
My breasts.
But no face.
My chemise, my garter, my blood, but nothing else of me.
Me. Reassembled like a chopped cadaver on the slab in
the morgue.
My anatomy triangulated and segmented, slotted into the
container of my padded cell.
No chance of marriage now...

The Baroness wore high heels and bedded her brother;
amongst other admirers. A true aristocrat.

When we were at Avignon, war was declared. Ironic.

Internally, my body was at war with itself and now the
disease was spreading, spreading...
Braque and Derain immediately decided to head for the
nearest mobilisation centre. Pablo took them to the station.
He never found them again.
Apollinaire applied for French citizenship, then joined up.
Almost everyone did.
Except Pablo.

Back in Paris the world had changed.
If we went to a cafe, the only men there were old or infirm.
Everyone would stare at him.
When he ordered, his French suddenly became halting,
confused, as if he had only just arrived here.
Not my war, he said. Not my war.

Ap joined the artillery. Poor Max was too unfit to join.
Kahnweiler had to flee the country, his assets were seized,
and so Pablo's paintings and the possibilities of sales...
vanished.
I told him to go to the bank: cash in hand was safer.
He did.

Time was beginning to slide away. I was coughing more
and more. Sharp pinpricks of pain in the chest.
Lack of energy. Pablo worked on collage, triangles of
plywood, marbled paper, newspaper cuttings, bric-a-brac
of all kinds, stuck, glued or tied: putting things together
as life falls apart.
I would cough my way to the window, 5 bis, Rue
Schoelcher, second floor, standing in the prow, staring
out over the cemetery.

I knew it by heart. Knew it as well as the images on the
studio walls: a window painting of the future as well as
of the past; a forest of small crosses, interspersed with
upright, cabined mausoleums and the occasional pillared
monument.

One fine sepulchre, carved from a polished and pinkish
marble, and topped with an urn, had a bronze palm leaf,
patinated with the sap of green...

Goldschmidt, Samama, Dreyfus, Israel...
Louis would have felt at home...

To the right was the *famille* Pinat, a cold blue-black
marble with a bronze sculpture of a young girl, standing
on tiptoe on the grave, offering upwards a posy of flowers
to the bust of a self-important man with eyebrows like the
grave and acute accent.

No chance of marriage now...
I had a servant to do the cleaning. Naturally I did most
of it myself.

It's cold, dark, everything is decaying. Zeppelins fly over
the city, sirens suddenly sound.
One's role... is... important.
Occasionally, when exhaustion crept away, we would
make a visit.
Not many to visit.
(*We hear Verdi's 'Teneste la Promessa. Play under.*)
Braque is a second-lieutenant. Derain is in a motorcycle
unit.
In the infantry, Ap is still falling off his horse.
Léger is at the front with the supply corps, brothers,
lovers, sons are frozen in the mud of trenches, and
Louis, my poor Louis, who volunteered for military
service, is God knows where.
He doesn't write to me.
Here in Paris, Juan Gris is starving, so Pablo won't be
visiting him.

Gertrude and Alice invite us over but the klaxon sounds
so Alice brings cushions, we crawl under the table, and
she lights a candle.

I am fatigued.
Pablo and Gertrude are yammering away. I am dying but
no comforting arm encases me, protects me from my fears.
Alice puts my head on the cushion and I try to sleep.
At two in the morning the alarm is over and we walk
back to the apartment.
Pablo is still yammering. I am silent with lost sleep.

Souvenirs arrive: a piece of shell-case, engraved by
Léger; a bullet from Apollinaire, from Braque an inkwell
made from a bit of tin hat. Amidst the darkness, Max,
poor gentle, lovable, boy-loving Max, having discussed
religion with Christ and the Blessed Virgin whom he met
at the cinema, discovers the one true Church and will be
baptised with Pablo as Godfather.
Braque is seriously wounded but Pablo doesn't write.
He makes a handsome pencil drawing of Max but he
never makes one of me.

No, he never makes one of me.
Instead, I cost him money. Doctor's bills. Then a private
clinic: hospitalised.
(*A dry laugh.*) The other side of Paris. Auteuil. 57 Avenue
de Montmorency.
He visits me every day, does Pablo, his devotion crossing
the metro like a metronome.
Just like his penis, crossing the street to meet Gaby
Lespinasse!
Pablo believed in regular exercise of all organs.
He exercised his representational wrist with portraits of
Vollard and Rosenberg, as well as Max. But then, they
could be of help to his career.
Whereas now, I was heading for infinity.

I used to sit in the clinic, imagining the cemetery in
Montparnasse.
There was a sentry-box sepulchre for the *famille*
Lefebvre. Inside, a tiny altar, flowers, and a prayer-stool
for kneeling.

The flowers were always fresh.
Would Pablo build me a sepulchre, erect an altar, bring
me fresh flowers as a gift of love?
Well... disappointed in life... disappointed in death...
(*Music fades.*)

It was a long, slow, cold trip to the cemetery. Max warmed
himself from his hip-pocket, cracked jokes, and made off
with the coachman. Pablo stared at my grave, then warmed
himself with Gaby Lespinasse.
And Louis?
Perhaps I freed him after all...
He finally did what he had always wanted to do...
just paint...
I would have made him a good wife. He would have
painted my portrait over and over, just to please me...
I could have lived, in your world, forever.
Could have... would have... but didn't.
Why... me?
Purposeless...

He never painted my portrait, did Pablo. Never even
drew me. Not a proper painting like those he did of
Fernande or Olga or Jacqueline. Not even a proper
drawing like those of almost every casual slut whose
legs he opened, for inspection with his pencil.
Only me, the ghost in the machine of his art... only me...
unmemorialised, unrecorded, unmade into art...

As the birdcage slowly rises into the Gods we hear Alfredo sing
Parigi, o cara, noi lasce remo from La Traviata. Just as Alfredo and
Violetta start to duet, EVA glides over to the swing and sits. Her
eyes travel upwards as the music swells, and the lights slowly fade to
blackness.

The End.

GABY

Unlike the other women in Picasso's life, Gaby seems to have decided, quite early on in the relationship, that life with Picasso was not worth the candle. With admirable perspicacity, she evaluated her options, and opted for safety – with another man. She was intelligent enough to know what she was losing, which makes her decision all the more courageous.

~

We hear John Cage's 'In a Landscape' echoing out of the darkness. It runs under the opening text. Light creeps onto the stage and during the following, the brittle good-time music of Poulenc or Milhaud fades in and out. The effect is surreal, haunting.

Stage right, light reveals Picasso's brightly-coloured Provençal Interior, Kitchen (or an image based on it), with its table laden with food, its open fireplace and its stairs leading to the bedroom. It is inscribed to GABY. The rear wall has the monochrome image of Herbert Lespinasse's wood-engraving Les Algues Brunes while stage left reveals Picasso's Provençal Interior, Bedroom, (or an image based upon it) which opens out onto a moonlit night, and which is also dedicated to GABY.

We find her, sitting with her back to us, staring at the Lespinasse image. She is hunched in concentration, her head slightly cocked as if her body were longing for a union no longer possible.

Swinging round to us.

GABY: Boxwood. Endgrain. Scraper. Wood-engraving.

As I lay dying, Herbert, my husband Herbert, read me
the pages of a William Faulkner novel. What novel?
Use your intelligence!
Herbert was an American, affluent, cultured of course,
surprisingly so for an American, who fell in love with
Paris, knew everyone, and enjoyed both the traditional
and the new. He read all the latest writers, had a sub-
scription to Transition, and there wasn't a decent painter
or printmaker in Montparnasse whom he didn't know.
So he read me *As I Lay Dying*.
He knew I wouldn't concentrate, just as he knew that I loved
the sound of his voice. If he was speaking English you
could hear his Stamford accent. When he spoke French,

it was the French of Montparnasse, elegantly phrased, precise, grammatically exact.

Pablo's was somewhat different.

Pablo thought in Spanish, translated into peculiar French like a boy construing a difficult passage, and spoke the elegant rhythms of my language with all the finesse of a butcher hacking at a cadaver.

But he was... Pablo...

(*Fade music.*)

So you are thinking, who am I, and who is Herbert? Not – who is Pablo... Some bookends to the footnotes of the Picasso story? Nonentities? Hangers-on to the Picasso legend?

Well... maybe footnotes... but we had sense.

Herbert was right.

He played the game, trusted me to make the right decision. And I did.

What decision you ask?

Simple: Pablo asked me to marry him.

Well... that is not quite correct. He asked me, then he begged me. Again and again.

And I refused.

But more of that later.

I was the first person he asked to marry him... but not the last!

You see, I wasn't quite like Pablo's other women.

Oh, I don't mean to acquire airs and graces but my family, while not being enormously rich, were more than comfortable. I had an allowance for those early years, my own flat in the Boulevard Raspail, top flat – fifth floor but my own flat – and when I first met Pablo I already knew Herbert; had even taken his name. So I had no absolute need to get a husband, no panicky thoughts as to where the next baguette was coming from, no need to bait a trap for lifelong security.

I was just being me.

Oh I know: you are asking yourselves: was she mad?
Why did she refuse the great God Pablo Picasso? Why
marry a nonentity like Herbert Lespinasse, an artist
whom most of the world has never heard of! Think of
the money, the fame...
Well, think of it indeed. You only need so much money
to stay alive. What use is the rest? Look at me. Do I look
as if you can take it with you?!
And fame. Well, what use is fame if it imprisons you?

I used to know a group of painters. Soutine. Modigliani.
Pascin. Utrillo.
They called them *Les peintres maudit.* Painters under
a curse.
Painters with a temper that could brim over into violence.
Painters to whom trouble came like flies to a flypaper.
Unhappy men, melancholic, irascible, awkward, gifted – but
most of the time they damaged only themselves.
But Pablo. He was different. Pablo took his demons and
impregnated his women with them. He put his women
under a curse. His curse.
He looked for a weakness, then like a little boy torturing
a butterfly by pulling off bits of its wings, he would wait
and watch to see how long it was before you would fail
to fly.
And when you failed to fly, you were of no further use.

But of course I speak in retrospect. Back then, I only had
pieces of the puzzle.

Boxwood. Endgrain. Scraper. Wood-engraving.
The colour of the best blocks is a deep and even yellow.
Somehow satisfying.
I once said to Herbert, it seems such a shame to make a
mark upon such a surface.
I could collect such blocks, re-arrange them as sculptures,

an endlessly changing sculpture to mirror our changing
lives!
He simply grinned... and told me to piss off!
And did you know: the best wood is imported from Turkey
and the Crimean.
My first lesson from Herbert: for the finest work, don't
use West Indian wood.
Too soft! Herbert was very particular about his blocks.
A craftsman. A professional.

As I lay dying, I started to ask myself questions. Well,
I was eighty-two. I had been with Herbert since 1914.
That's fifty-six years! Not bad for a relationship,
considering what we got up to! But more of that later!
What was I saying?
As I lay dying.
Yes. Questions. Well, you do ask yourself questions,
don't you?
Was it all worth it? Did I make any major mistakes?
Is there a life after death? Should I have had the cat
neutered? Should I have married Pablo? Should I have
had such a good time when I was young?
Well, you know how people frown upon promiscuity
these days, don't you. And I had more fucks than there
are hatchings in one of Herbert's wood-engravings.
Mind you, the same applied to Herbert, and Pascin, and
Kisling, and Kiki and Nils, and just about anybody who
went round with us. I suppose, in a way, we were all a
bit like Pablo: only we grew up, eventually, and he
never did!

Yes, I know. You want to hear about me and Pablo. (*Beat.*)
Tough!
I'm telling this story. It's my life, so I get to do the
'deconstructing'. It's the one great thing about being dead
– and don't let anyone ever tell you otherwise – you can't
be contradicted. Ignored, forgotten, desired maybe,
but never contradicted. Now Pablo. He would have
contradicted the pope – after he'd blessed himself

and swallowed a bottle of holy water.
By the way, there is one great big problem about being
dead: you can't have sex.
You can think about it. But you can't do it.
So I don't recommend the experience.
You'll find out soon enough anyway.
So where was I? Pablo, sex, and the pope.
Yes, Pablo.
1915.

I first met him in *La Rotonde*. Then it was a small
cafe, not far from the intersection of the Raspail and
Montparnasse boulevards. The *patron*, who used to be a
butcher, was old Leblanc. It was wartime and most
artists had cold ateliers, little coal or gas, and few
blankets. You could sit all day over your *café crème* and
get your *choucroute* or soup on credit and if you had the
skill you could draw soldiers, who were on leave, from
the front. They were always willing to pose.
A free model!
At night came the bourgeois, and the bohemians.
I could be both. So could Herbert. Bohemian or bourgeois.

Pablo didn't like soldiers. Once or twice I saw him
glance in the window, see a uniform, then turn and
stride off. Being young, and fit, he had no wish to be
stared at – accusingly... Guilt was a novel experience for
Pablo – novel and disturbing. (*Beat.*)
It was January, 1915. Night time. I was with Herbert.
We were dining well, downing the wine, laughing. I was
twenty-seven years old.
If I looked around I could see elderly civil servants, en
route from the office, placid businessmen with their placid
wives, and handsomely over-painted ladies, waiting
patiently for a client.

I didn't notice him come in but I felt his gaze.
When I turned round, he was staring at me: large,
luminous eyes. Stocky. An English cap on the table.

A quiff of thick black hair almost down to his
eyebrow. And a slow, easy smile as his eyes caught
mine.
I recognised those eyes.
Bedroom eyes.
Eyes that undressed you on first acquaintance.
Eyes that slid up your legs and entered you.
Dangerous eyes.

I fluttered my eyelashes – just enough to let him know that
I found his gaze to be – shall we say – stimulating, then
I ignored him for the rest of the night. Herbert, who was a
shrewd observer, was well aware. He told me, a lop-sided
grin upon his big gangly frame, 'Your new admirer, seeing
you in your scanties I'll bet. That's Picasso.
He's a biggie. No shortage of big bills there. Better
artist.'
One of Herbert's traits. No false modesty. He knew
himself and his limitations.
And he knew me.

Sometimes we'd go to Marie Wassilieff's.
She was a dumpy little Russian who started out running
a soup kitchen in her atelier for indigent artists and
writers. Soon it became the place.
A three course meal for sixty-five centimes.
But it wasn't only the poor who went. If you wanted to
meet artists of any kind, then you went to Marie's.
Herb never actually ate there. But as it stayed open long
after curfew, officially not serving wine or spirits – which
naturally it did – we all got shellacked there. Preferably
on wine.

Modigliani, Modo we called him, between cadging drinks
and smoking his little pellets of hash... God he was such a
handsome man, flawless features, dark passionate eyes...
would be dreamily stripping off, admiring himself in his
own reflection, until, entirely naked, he would swirl round
and round, sliding to a floor or a lap.

It was there I saw Pablo again. There were drawings by
him on the wall.
Not particularly interesting.

And he had every intention of being a centre of
attention. His game was to be a bull. Max Jacob would
snatch up a tablecloth and throw it to him. Pablo, head
erect, chest puffed out, Max's walking stick stuck
through his belt, would prance up and down between
the tables. Some shellacked girl, her rump waggling,
bent over, tongue lolling, fingers in her ears, would
make an impassioned charge and the maestro himself,
cocky on tiptoe, would plunge his protuberance into
her quivering flanks.
Then, his foot upon her supine flank, protuberance
upraised, he would give a low sweeping bow, rising to
the cheering thunder of fists on tables.

He caught me looking at him, an expression of amused
dismissal upon my face.
His face... fell...
Then, one night, I was at Hélène's. Without Herbert.

You've heard of Hélène? The Baroness D'Oettingen.
Pablo knew her well. No riff-raff in her circle.
He was sitting there as I entered.
It was as if I could see myself undressing in the mirrors
of his eyes.
He really was a most attractive man.
Like all men accustomed to power, and what is a great
artist but a man of unlimited power, tightly cocooned in
prestige and – if in addition he has the gift of sale-ability
– then, like Pablo, he knows that his mere presence
mesmerizes. He knows that he can have what he wants.
Knows that he can click his fingers and his acolytes will
hand over their wives and mistresses, like sweetmeats,
waiting to be sucked and savoured.

I told him to fuck off.
Oh it was such a pleasure to see his cock wilt in
his trousers.
He simply couldn't believe it.
Listen – and I'm talking to you women now – with men
like Pablo, it is important to realise that the woman must
be strong, independent, take no nonsense. Otherwise such
men assume divinity in themselves. You are there for the
taking; and the discarding. Whereas, with men like Pablo,
it is you who should take – and discard.

So I walked off, half turning to display my rump to best
advantage – one should always give them a hint of what
they are missing!
Of course, I knew most of the people in the room,
including Irène Lagut towards whom our wilted cock
made haste. He needed to assure himself that he still
had the power but Irène was Serge's mistress, Serge
being the so-called brother of the Baroness, so he could
hardly try a seduction in situ! (*Beat.*)
I was enjoying myself.
Observing him obliquely. How long before our
wilting wallflower would cockify himself into a
strutting hoofer.
The English – appalling race – have a phrase for people
like Pablo: cuntstruck.
Herbert, who enjoyed words, and published poetry in the
little magazines, gleefully told me once that it was army
slang for men who saw women as vulvas, and who were
hooked on fucking.
Pure Pablo.

I watched him, watching every man who came up to me.
How his eyes narrowed if they rested their hand on
the bare flesh of my arm. How his lips thinned if some
friend should put an arm around my shoulders and
kiss me gently – well, with just a little tonguing! His
whole body seemed to grit itself, and now he held his legs

tightly together. So I knew it was only a matter of time. I
went over and kissed Irène. So what is this man like I ask,
and whom is he with? And doesn't it turn out that he's
been living with a woman I knew slightly, called Eva. But
seemingly she's very ill. And so the matador has come out
to play!

Boxwood. Endgrain. Scraper. Wood-engraving.

Before beginning work, one prepares the smooth block,
rubbing down the surface with damp powdered bath-brick,
ever so carefully, until one has a slightly matt surface.
'Giving it a slight tooth' was Herbert's expression.
I had given Pablo a slight tooth, hadn't I! Now it was the
time to let him dangle. Pablo wasn't going to add me to
his collection. I was going to add him to mine...
He kept finding a pretext for coming up to me. I allowed
myself to be introduced to him. By the end of the night
I had him nicely trained.
Remember. If all you want is a good time, a pleasant
fling with a man who has money, power and reputation,
then instigate Gaby's Art of Training Men.
Immediately.

Men are like dogs and they train just as easily. A
little petting here, a little withholding there, a brisk
flick across the nose, and the tone – the tone is
all-important. You must never, ever allow yourself to
become submissive.
You may open your legs, but if he doesn't do what
you want, then whip him with words until he's like a
beaten cur, whimpering in the corner, waiting on a
kind word.
Of course, this is only for short-term relationships.
The longer ones need a different strategy.

Pablo had a problem: Eva. Obviously it was inadvisable
for a dying woman to find out that her lover was shagging

an acquaintance of hers. This suited me fine. I had no wish
to embarrass Herbert either. We had an open relationship
but there are courtesies.
Pablo's desire for secrecy was almost amusing.
After a few weeks he presented me with a drawing.
Naturally it is of himself.
He is standing at the crossroads between the boulevard
Edgar Quinet and Boulevard Raspail, a pipe jutting out
of his mouth, cap in one hand, and a box of chocolates in
the other. Behind him a dog is amusing itself on the
pavement and fat little Diego Rivera is waddling towards
him in the distance.
He is waiting for me to signal that the coast is clear so
that he can come up to my apartment. Naturally I keep
him waiting, especially as he doesn't like Diego.

Now, be honest. What are you thinking? This woman is
a slut, a tramp, someone who toys with the affections
of others?
Actually not. People like Pablo are sluts. But he is a man so
he gets away with it. Do I not speak the truth?

Back then, we lived in a very free-and-easy time. We
took our pleasures as and when we wanted to. Moïse,
Moïse Kisling that is, Moïse of the smooth olive skin
and beautiful black eyes, another artist of course, and a
friend, enjoyed women.
Painted society women as well as models – patting them
on the thighs and back as if they were fine mares.
They rarely took it amiss.

Pascin, in his black felt hat with the snap brim, whose
exquisite sensuality seeped into his portraits and whose
urgent eye turned sharp for the vivid pleasure of a fine leg
or a delicate profile, once casually remarked that 'the
moment of ejaculation cannot be abstracted'.

Kiki, perhaps the most famous artist's model in the
whole of Montparnasse, posed nude for Man Ray,

wearing only a turban, and with the sound holes of a violin superimposed on her slender back. He called it *Violin d'Ingres*, slang for a hobby or a pastime – which she was.

We all were. We were experimenting. No need to take anything, or anyone, too seriously.

You see, that was the secret. If you were sensible, you had a good time.

Made whoopee. Explored the male, excavated the species, weighed up the pros and cons, and then figured out whom you could *live* with.

You needed experience – and you needed judgement. The trick was not to think that you had fallen in love just because the body was beautiful, or the sex was stunning, or the strokes of his paintbrush had smoothed your imperfections into seductive and flattered flesh.

Not many of us managed the trick, perhaps... but I did. I turned Pablo down, and of course I anticipate, but my instincts were right. You remember me mentioning Irène, Serge's mistress? Now Irène was beautiful, and wanton and reckless, and thank – I was about to say thank God but it should be thanks to her good sense – finally sensible.

When I turned Pablo down, turned down his offer of marriage that is, he decided that Irène should be his wife. So he laid siege to her, and at one point kidnapped her and held her prisoner for a week, locking her in a room at his house in Montrouge. She escaped so he stole a nude photograph of her, blackmailed her, telling her that either she would be his wife, or else he would tell Serge who did not consider photographs to be art. She refused, so Pablo went to Serge's sister, showed him the photograph and said Irène was a whore, that he had been fucking her, and that she was anybody's.

Nice man, eh?

But you never know at the start, do you? You only see the gifts, the smiles, the endearments. You don't want to know, do you? Always you are thinking: this will be... perfection... You find a hundred excuses for every lapse. Your ingenuity is such that you could take up a career as a novelist, exploring the motivations, the anxieties, the little tics of your protagonist. You want to understand him, don't you? And of course, aren't you the only one who can unlock the cabinet of his heart...
Ahhhh!

Okay. Hands up. How many of you think that you really know that man beside you? Hmmm?
How many of you think that you are his one and only love? Not a lot.
How many of you think he's fucking someone else on the side?
Has fucked someone else?
Will fuck someone else?
Now what does that tell you?

Don't look at me! I'm deconstructing my life and that's quite enough as it is!

So where were we?
Boxwood. Endgrain. Wood-engraving.

What was it that Herbert liked about wood-engraving? Oddly enough, the drama. In most ways he was a quiet man, laid-back, easy-going, relaxed – but he knew exactly what he wanted. I used to watch him, sitting in a corner by the window, with his piece of boxwood on the table.
Every cut had to be final, deliberate, irrevocable. There was no room for mistakes.
The image had to be worked out exactly, in the head, or on paper, before you started. That was Herbert.
He always liked to have things worked out, but without you knowing it.

A good psychologist. Unlike Pablo.
Pablo put his psychology into his work. Herbert put it
into the handling of people.
No drama.
Herbert put that into his work.
Intense blacks and pure whites in dramatic opposition.
Yet lines, tones and gradations of great subtlety... he
really was... such a subtle man.
He knew that I was seeing Pablo. But he said nothing.
I told him I was going away for three or four days.
He knew what I was up to.

Herbert, after all, had a house in Saint-Tropez, beside the
beach on the Baie des Canoubiers. In the twenties, didn't
we all go there for months on end, Kisling, Pascin, Kiki,
Nils, anyone who was anyone, provided they were painters
or writers, wives or girlfriends, or simply supporters of the
arts, all of us down to lead the good life, soaking in the
Mediterranean sun, scavenging on the beach for
driftwood, lounging down to a stream or well for water,
and fishing for lunch. Not to mention sketching, painting,
writing, composing the odd concerto, having sex... but
more of that later.

You younger generations get so easily excited...

Well, just a little hint.
Herbert, in the mid-morning sun, standing on the
beach, nude. Beside him, Nils, equally nude, equally
standing on the beach. Both of them, practising their
golf swing. I could never get interested in golf. But
every now and then myself, Nils's wife or whomever
happened to be there, would pull the curtains at the
window and stand there, calling until they heard us.
Then we'd wait and see how long it took before they
had two erect tools in their hands.
See what you're missing!

I know. Back to Pablo. Everyone wants to hear about
Pablo.
I took him to Saint-Tropez. Had a key.
He'd never been there.

Imagine the coastline: Marseille, Toulon, Le Lavandrou,
Saint-Tropez, then Saint-Raphael, Cannes, Nice and
Monaco. Of course nowadays the entire coast is packed
with daubers, armed with palettes and idiocy. Naturally
the landowners have resorted to sticking up huge signs
declaring 'Painters Prohibited'! And in the shooting
season, anything lurking behind an easel is fair game.
Elsewhere the neon lights of casinos glitter and gleam
amidst the stucco corridors.
No longer Provence, except on a map.
Just an outpost of New York, Amsterdam, Berlin or Paris.

But when we first went there, it was another world. Corot
and Boudin had journeyed through, producing the odd
picturesque scene but Herbert was one of the first to live
there, long before it was fashionable for the likes of Matisse
and Marquet, Bonnard and Lebasque.
Pablo knew a good thing when he saw it. From cloudy
Northern skies to a vast aerial space, the light lustrous,
crystalline and sparkling... from the dull red brick of
Paris to the translucent brick of Saint-Tropez, glowing
under a glittering sun... the blue shoreline waters with
their shimmering hues and the steep rocky hills, stained
like old marble with the rust of ages, catching fire in the
radiance of the afternoon.
Tall spires of cypress would cast motionless shadows and in
the sheltered ripeness of the shoreline areas, groves of
lemon and orange would gloss into yellow-green and scent
the evening breeze.

No hordes of baying tourists! Only the occasional
motor-car with its tootling klaxon.
Peace and tranquillity.

Living was... cheap! Money wasn't a problem.
Youth had its own easy assurance, with a garnish
of carelessness.

He painted me, nude, in the garden, splayed out against
the background of Roman-tiled rooves, cypresses, and
far-off hills. Everything was a prelude to sex. If I lay on
the beach, languorous in the mid-day sun, I became a
photograph, legs curving, rhyming with an upraised arm,
a svelte sinuosity of flesh, an entry in his notebook of
future plans. If we went sight-seeing, to the village of
Ramatuelle with its abandoned windmills, he would want
to roll me in the scrub and take me there and then. In
Cogolin, where Herbert had bought a blue-and-white rug
for the house, he would puff on his pipe, then stop at one
of the hole-in-the-wall workshops where the peasants
make briar pipes, carving strange shapes suggested by
the bend and twist of the wood.

Then the bowl would be drilled out, the mouthpiece gently
fashioned and the whole polished into a richly-grained
sculptural pipe.

Pablo would be fascinated, intrigued by the skill, wanting to
try it for himself. You know the great thing about pipes, he
asked me? You suck on them like a tit, and you poke with
them like a penis! And he would make a gesture with his
pipe, and the gap-toothed old peasants would screech with
laughter, and then Pablo would smile broadly, and leer at
me, King Midas amidst his congregation, and I would lean
forward to the peasants and in a loud whisper I'd casually
say, 'I really like to be masturbated,' whereupon Pablo
would haul me out of the way, jabbering about decency
and what-not.

Men are such hypocrites!

He never quite could fathom me, could Pablo. He kept
on expecting that I would bow to his will. After the first
day in Saint-Tropez, he casually tossed down a copy of
the Marquis de Sade. *Juliette*, I think. I offered to tie him
up and stick pins in his penis.

He whitened. Visibly.

Strange, isn't it: he had never actually considered that
the sadism might be applied to himself!
I told him that I had read the book when I was fifteen,
and gave him a lecture on the modern readings of de Sade
in relation to Freud.
That stopped him talking about de Sade.

But I would have to say that the man had his points.
He knew everyone.
We would be lying on the bed, him trying to undress me,
teasing me, telling me stories, making me laugh.
How he used to walk with Eric Satie all the way to
Auteuil. A two-hour walk.
And he would imitate Satie, walking like a little civil
servant with a bowler hat and a belly and a very large
umbrella. Show me how the plump little composer carried
a hammer in his pocket to protect himself from attack.
Demonstrate how Satie would hum to himself, composing
as he waddled along.
Act out how he, Pablo, would fight off the footpads
who had foregathered to steal the fifty centimes in
Satie's pockets!

And then he could be... oh so gentle. He knew a woman's
body with the precision of a map maker and the skills of a
midwife. He could make you squeak and squeal or squelch
and scream. He could make you sing with the purity of one
of those operatic castrati.
He could make you moan softly, sliding you into sleep
on his strong broad chest.
Oh, yes: he was a good fuck.

Don't look so surprised. If a man says it, everybody nods
and flexes their wrists.
Women aren't supposed to think like that.
Bollocks!
But remember the trick! Never believe that a good fuck
is akin to love.
The one has no necessary correlation to the other.

It's just that we always like to think otherwise...

Pablo was fine when he was trying to please. When
he was making an effort. And he made an effort for
me. He was besotted. He wanted to possess me, to take
me over, to put me into a little box and gloat over me.
To take me out whenever it suited him. To fuck me
whenever he felt the need – if he was becoming bored,
or irritated, or if he couldn't sleep. He would never
understand that I had no intention of becoming
subservient. Why should I be an appendage when
I could be an equal?
Why should I want to become another Eva?

As I lay dying...
Hah!
As I lay dying, didn't Herbert lean forward once and ask
me, very quietly, did I regret choosing him instead
of Pablo?
His face was lined and creased, cleft by deep gorges,
seamed by dry torrent beds.
The colour of brick red.
As I looked out the window in the back room of our
house in Saint-Tropez, it was as if he had become one of
those steep rocky hills.
He felt that he had let me down.
We had little money, almost all of our friends had died –
I shushed him.
Smiled until he bent a little nearer. 'No regrets my love...'
I pushed my arm around his scrawny neck, and felt the
last flickerings of an evening sun. 'You've held me every
day for fifty-seven years. Taken care of me. Loved me.
Pablo would never have done that.'
And I died as I lay there, cradled in his strong scrawny
arms.

(*We hear Satie's Three Gymnopédies creep in.*)
It was in this bed... Pablo and me... he had given me a
necklace made out of wooden beads, each one painted by
himself with little geometrical motifs.

I used to wear it, and nothing else.
We would be in the kitchen. That one.
(*Pointing to the image stage right.*)
I'd be making dinner... he'd be sketching me... having lit
the fire so I could cook... often, I'd no sooner get a
cassoulet on the hob than I'd feel his tongue sliding in
and he'd be muttering 'Dessert before dinner! Dessert
before dinner!'
... And I liked dessert...

It was an... idyll. (*Points to the wall again.*)
We were only away for four days.
When we got back he gave me that watercolour. He had
written a long inscription. It said: 'Gaby, my love... the
little staircase is the way to your bedroom. You're my
life, you, you my sweetness, I love you, I am so happy to
be with you, my angel. Always, and for all days, the only
thing I ask is to be able to write to you. I love you with
all the colours.'
And then he printed 'I Love You' six different times in
six different colours.
Not forgetting the signature.

Strange, isn't it, how such an intelligent man could write
such crap.
Thirty-five years old. And writing like a schoolboy
scrawling graffiti on a wall.
Now Herbert was a poet. He appreciated words. He would
never have written 'my angel... my sweetness, you're my
life, I am so happy to be with you...'
And why?
Because they're insincere, stock phrases, they tell us
nothing about Pablo, or me, or his love. They just tell us
that Pablo used flattery to try and get what he wanted.

He gave me a steady stream of watercolours, all with
similar declarations of undying love, all little more than
conventional lies.
I said earlier that he wasn't a very good psychologist.

Not quite true. He was when it came to sex and other men.
My watercolours were beautiful but Pablo was painting
Herbert's house. Herbert's earthenware pots, Herbert's
Cogolin rug, Herbert's Provençal chests... and Herbert's
bed with the moon gleaming brightly in the deep
blue night.
He didn't have to paint me in the bed.
He reckoned that any man couldn't help but think of
him... Picasso... having his woman. It was a little edge
that he wanted...
But he was charming as he gave them, and a little bit of
me wanted to believe, wanted to think that this 'great man'
really did find me special; really did wish to spend the
rest of his days ensconced only with me.

He gave me a long decorative panel, brightly-coloured
like the Provençal memories, with abstract decorations
like those on my necklace. One panel said, in big blue
letters, 'Your Love is for me My Life' and another had
my name in blue intertwined with his in orange.
Then came his *pièce de resistance*: four tiny oval watercolours, two tiny oval photographs (one of me, one of
him), and a decorative panel with I Love You Gaby and
our intertwined names, all mounted against a black
background and framed.
Three of the watercolours were of pretty little flowers,
sheet music, and a mandolin.
The fourth showed a naked me, in bed, with a little
naked cherub flying overhead and closing the curtain.
At the bottom, he had written in black ink on white
paper 'I've asked the Good God for your hand, Paris
22nd February, 1916'.

Pablo had just left my apartment. His 'proposal' was
propped against the wall.
I left it there.
When Herbert came up later on that night, he examined
it closely.

'Kinda decorative cubism', he said. 'I kinda like the little cherub.'

I went into my bedroom, pulled a small portfolio from under the bed, and showed him the other watercolours.

'Well, well', he drawled, 'so he wants to make my place famous!'

He didn't mention the proposal.

I handed him the portfolio, heaved up the framed work, and dropped it into his arms.

He looked at me. Curious.

'A present', I said.

'Who for?'

'My husband', I said softly.

We married on April the 23rd, 1917, at Saint-Tropez. Pablo had been sending me drawings with 'Come back my love, my angel' written on them in large letters. 'Don't think much of his prose style', said Herbert, chuckling as he put them into the portfolio. 'You never know. Might be our pension plan some day!'

April 23, 1917.

Herbert invited Pablo to the wedding but, as anticipated, he didn't come.

It wouldn't have mattered if he had. We were strong enough to survive him.

We always had an open house at Saint-Tropez... wives, mistresses, artists, writers.

Herbert loved naked female bodies and I loved firm naked males. We all got along.

If someone made a scene, became possessive, then they weren't invited back.

But that was rare.

We simply enjoyed ourselves, renewed ourselves, skinny-dipped on the beach, delighted in the exploration of new bodies – and always we had each other to return to.

A month after the wedding – we had stayed at Saint-Tropez – came *La Bravade*, the annual fete. It lasts for

three days, and the town is alive with banners and
flowers, fife and drum.
In the church there is a bust of Saint Torpes, a Christian
martyr who was beheaded, set adrift in a boat and then
washed up in what became our Saint-Tropez.

Everyone dresses up, the crowds surge to the church, and
the beribboned and beflowered bust of Saint Torpes is
carried through the streets, as the bells peal, down to the
Quai where the sailors fire a salute for the saint, before
carrying the bust back to the church.
Then the dancing starts and lasts till dawn.

Every year, during *La Bavade*, I always thought of Pablo.
Amidst the music and the dancing and the cheering crowds
I would see the bust of Saint Torpes... but it would be
Pablo's head, silently mouthing, 'Gaby, come back to me
Gaby, come back!'
And then I would seem to see these women, like the
tricoteuses at the Guillotine, emerging like shadows from
the crowd. They would line up in front of the head, and
then one of them would lean forward, a needle and thread
in her hand, and sew up his mouth.
And I would see his eyes, silently imploring me, and
I would hear one of the women silently say, 'What use
are words, if you don't mean them?' And then his
image would fade, and I would turn around, and there
would be Herbert, slipping his arm through mine,
urging me to dance.

Boxwood. Endgrain. Scraper. Wood-engraving.

As I lay dying, (*She gestures towards Herbert's image on the
back wall.*) I used to stare at Herbert's art, mounted on
the wall.
Lines, specks, hatchings and stipples.
I could see in his hands the gravers, spitstickers, scorpers
and chisels.

I could hear him talk about how he had to find an equivalent mark, a way of translating, roundness and sleekness, roughness and softness, into the printing surface of close-grained wood.

How many times did I hear him say that unlike a painter, he produced no mess, no smell, no noise.

Give him an hour and he could get something done. He could take up the block and put down the block at any stage, without having to worry.

No need for prolonged, uninterrupted attention.

Unlike Pablo.

And so... he had time for me...

Not like Pablo...

Strange, isn't it...

I lied, of course, to Herbert. About Pablo.

About choosing him instead of Pablo.

One always regrets what might have been.

One always likes to have a little... indulgence... a little secret compartment, in the cabinet of the heart, where one can dream of what might have been.

And yet I know, if I had chosen Pablo, he would have deconstructed me like one of his cubist portraits. Without mercy.

And that is why, of course, I felt free to dream.

I just walked away... lived a full, round life... and what do I resent?

Just one thing.

That people know me as Pablo's one-time mistress... not as Herbert's wife...

(*The John Cage 'In a Landscape' plays as she slowly swivels round to face Herbert's wood-engraving, and then as the stage lights begin to slowly fade to darkness, segue into an American Flapper-style tune. She is smiling.*)

The End.

OLGA

Olga considered herself to be of the Russian nobility. Even Picasso, late on in life, considered her to be a 'real lady' with excellent social connections. There is however no Kokhlova family in the Russian equivalent of Debrett. Her father's background was military, and it's not perhaps too far-fetched to see that aspect emerge in her organisational skills and her single-mindedness.

She's had a bad press. John Richardson, one of the major Picasso biographers, castigates her as 'being silly and irredeemably square... infatuated and jealous to the point of insanity'. About the only canard not thrown at her is the accusation of promiscuity (routinely used to tar the other women). We are told that she's average, boring, insensitive, ignorant, an inept ballet-dancer etc. etc.

However when one starts to sift actual evidence, most of these accusations melt away. Rather more interestingly, if one attempts to look at the world from her point of view, a rather different version of events emerges.

Obviously this is my Olga. There is no absolute need for the actress playing her to ape a Russian accent. It's her character and her story that matter and the occasional phrases will 'place' her. (She knew Spanish, French and a smattering of Polish and English.) She knew her place in society (marriage, even if the husband had decamped), and like DORA she was almost un-doubtedly pushed over the edge into psychotic disturbances. It is my belief that the blame for this resides fairly and squarely with Picasso. It is also my belief that this woman had much more to offer – and was much more intelligent – than is generally credited.

Her voice can shift from languorousness to acidity without taking a breath; from a purring velvety sheen to a strident sandpapery rasp. This is a voice whose every modulation betokens control, and precision, even in the height of anger. She can say 'shit' and make you think it's part of a natural, aristocratically polite, vocabulary. This is also a voice that has insulated itself against its deepest wellspring: passion... but it's a wellspring that gears in and out of her two 'voices', that of the dead Olga, and that of the Olga in any specific time or place.

~

A burst of Shostakovich, perhaps his <u>Twelfth Symphony</u> (celebrating the Russian Revolution), or else the <u>Fifteenth Symphony</u> with its vitality and somewhat enigmatic humour. The music stops abruptly: the light suddenly finds OLGA, heading straight for us.

OLGA: You listening? Oi! You!
Well who do you think I'm talking to?
Some people!
(*Reasonably.*) Being dead: you think that's an advantage?
You think I *want* to talk to you.
(*Unexpectedly.*) I do, actually.
(*Garrulous.*) One serious advantage, being dead, is you got a whole world to talk to. Millions, trillions, zillions of 'em.
Course, talking to dead people, that's no joke. Who wants to talk to a disembodied corpse?
You think I want to talk philosophy? Who gives two shits about Ockam's Razor, darling? You think I want to talk to rabble? To academics? I got shoals of 'em up here, art critics, reviewers, biographers, crap artists all of 'em, all of 'em wanting to talk Picasso!
(*With energy.*) Stuff Pablo! Haven't I had enough of that whinging, whining, sarcastic, sadistic, sex-fixated night-mare?
Anal retentive!

Me, I want to talk to someone intelligent, a good listener, someone with a bit of wit. Like you.
Someone who's got an open mind.
Not like those... those clots who wrote about Pablo... and me! You listen to them, you think I'm insufferable.
(*Reasonably.*) OK. I *am* insufferable.
(*With a louring vehemence.*) Now!
He drove me to it! You think I *wanted* to be insufferable?
Does any woman want to be insufferable? Does any woman want to lose her husband, lose her position, lose her mind?

Cobcém Het. ('Course not.)
Listen to those critics though – hah! – you'd think I was thick as two party apparatchiks! (*Reasonably.*) I speak Russian, I speak French, I speak Spanish, I even speak a little English, I can read Polish.
(*With ironic sweetness.*) So what do they tell you? Average, they say. I'm average, frowsy and freckled... all but illiterate.

They'll tell you I knew nothing about art, nothing about music, nothing about literature.

Is that so! (*Light as a soufflé.*)
If it wasn't for the fact that up here there's nothing to get hold of, I'd take the Eiffel Tower, and each of those male backsides, and I'd show you what an enema is!!
(*Screams.*) Piss-artists the lot of 'em!
Now Pablo. *He* knew nothing about music. Told Stravinsky before Stravinsky found him out. (*Imitates Picasso's lousy accented French.*) '*He ne suis pas musicien, he comprends rien dans la musique.*'
Rien is right. Couldn't follow two bars unless he was walking from one to the other!
And as for literature, hah! The only time Pablo opened a book was to look at the pictures.

(*Sulkhan Tsintsadze. Miniatures for String Quartet. No.1. Indi-Mindi.*)
(*With pride.*) My papa however was rich and powerful and cultured, a colonel in the artillery under the Tzar Nicolas.
We were from a noble family.
Papa would visit Shchukin in Moscow: *the* Shchukin. So I would visit Shchukin– *the* Shchukin, the Shchukin who would return from Paris with paintings by Matisse and Picasso and Bonnard.
(*Fade out music.*)

I saw the work of the best of our contemporaries:
Grigoriev, Exter, Archipenko. Discussed their works with Tatlin, Kandinsky, Malevich and Schukkaev.
(*Offhandedly.*) We might consider the stories of Turgenev, the novels of Fyodor Mikkailovich Dostoyevsky – his father was murdered by peasants on his farm you know – and the poetry of Pushkin, or the early work of Count Aleksey Nikolayevich Tolstoy.

(*A touch of warmth creeps in.*) Or we would listen to the symphonies of Balakiref, Tchaikovsky, Arensky or Rimsky-Korsakof.

Proper Russian composers!

(*Sounds of a beach. We are on the Riviera in the 1940's: the soft lapping of the waves, the occasional breeze, the skirl of a gull, the distant sounds of children playing – and the hot sunshine.*)
(*Elegiacally.*) I had a life... then... but I became... her!!!
(*She becomes the warring harridan, well into her fifties, determined to be noticed, determined to take over the beach.*)
(*To no one in particular.*) Nice day. Nice beach. Nice breeze, don't you think?
(*Pleased with herself.*) Think I'll sit here.
Well Paulo, you can see that I'm here. I want to talk to your father, I'm going to talk to your father. I have something of the highest importance to tell him.
Why is he turning his back on me? That's not very nice of him, is it Paulo?
(*Spitting it out.*) Typical.

(*Calling.*) Picasso! Piss-artist!
(*Confidentially.*) I have to speak to you about your son. Getting old are we Pablo, gone deaf are we Pablo, gone back to babysnatching have we Pablo?
(*Calling out.*) Françoise! How delightful to see you, and nice little baby Claude. Isn't it nice to know that at his age, Pablo managed to get it up at least once!
(*Confidentially.*) You sure it's yours Pablo?

(*Grumpily.*) I don't know how he can go on pretending that I'm not here Paulo. Your father never could face up to anything... unpleasant! For God's sake tell your father that I must talk to him. It's very urgent!!
(*Sweetly. Calling.*) Pablo, my sweet, my little dove, my little fat friend, you're combing your hair over your bald patch Pablo. I could put a cockroach in between the gaps!
(*Aggressively.*) You haven't paid the hotel bill Pablo! I've been living in one since 1935, Pablo so you haven't exactly forgotten the address, have you Pablo? You haven't paid me anything in three months!

(*Sweetly.*) We have a legal agreement Pablo so either you pay me or I'll take one of your easels and ram it up your nostrils!

¿*Entiendo*? (Understand?)
¿*Que le vamos a hacer*? (What are we going to do about it?)
No hay tiempo que perder. (There is no time to lose.)
You'll have to learn Spanish, Françoise! (*Tartly.*) I'll buy you a phrase book.
(*Formally.*) *Puis-je vous présenter mon mari Françoise?* (May I introduce my husband?)
(*With satisfaction.*) You'll observe Françoise that he still wears my wedding ring. *Our* wedding ring. He'll never stop wearing it Françoise.
(*With lofty formality.*) *Voici mon fils Paulo. Ça va Françoise?* (This is my son Paulo. Right Françoise?)
(*Needling.*) Marie-Thérèse had a son Françoise: but he's not legitimate, is he Françoise?
Nice baby Claude. But you'd have to marry Pablo, Françoise, if he's to be legitimate... Rather difficult, don't you think as he's still legally married to me...

(*A gull squalls in triumph. As she half turns we hear a stinging slap across the face, and see her body react. For a few seconds she is in shock. Then she recovers and a slow smile spreads across her face. She inclines towards the audience.*)
(*Elegiacally.*) He never did divorce me. He wore our ring until the day he died and Paulo was the only son that he ever regarded as legitimate.
(*Shafting.*) Deep down, the bastard loved me. He just didn't show it.
(*A beat.*) Once, they were coming back from the beach. He still hadn't paid me. So I tugged at his arm and –
(*Astonished.*) He hit me... I screamed, started crying, and he says, the big bully, if you keep this up, I'll call for the police.
(*In genuine surprise.*) Keep what up?
(*In pain.*) Why does he tell Paulo when and where he's

going on holiday if he doesn't want me to come?
Why doesn't he just send me a cheque every month
instead of making me beg for it like a dog?
(*Aggressively.*) Well? Come on! Answer me! You're not
dumb... oh, I know what you're thinking. You're thinking:
not very *bright* Olga... not very bright.
I was... *un...* hinged... I was baggage and bones... I was like
one of Pablo's paintings, re-arranged, drained, stripped
and framed, a carcass pinned to the wall. I was a freckled
eggshell, with the yolk sucked out.
So I told her.

(*Street noise, late 1940's, Riviera. Perhaps a car. OLGA runs after
(the unseen) FRANÇOISE. We hear a key inserted into a lock.*)
(*Shouting.*) Coee Françoise! You stole my husband
Françoise! This is *my* house Françoise.
(*Running up out of breath.*) My *husband* lives there!

And I pinched her, scratched at her, pushed and pulled
her, slapped her!
They were staying at Monsieur and Madame Fort's. He
used to be Vollard's printer. *She* was nice. Came to the
door. *She* knew Picasso's wife. 'I'd be delighted to have tea
with you,' I said, squeezing my way past that strumpet.
So I did.
Every day.

If someone came to call on Pablo, I'd say 'My husband
isn't here. He's away for the afternoon. I'm back living
with him as you can see!'

(*A brief touch of Bortnyansky's <u>Song of the Cherubim</u>.*)
(*With delicate warmth.*) I wrote to him, almost every day.
He needed me to tell him what a shit he was.
Revenge and virtue, rolled into one. (*With satisfaction.*)
Neat! (*Amused.*) And I'd toss in bits of Russian and
Spanish, that way Françoise wouldn't understand! *Très,
très* neat!
(*Bluntly.*) You've got it I trust?

We women need to stick together – unless you're called Fernande, or Françoise, or Dora, or Jacqueline, or Marie-Thérèse...

(*Triumphantly.*) You see, Pablo was a hoarder! Couldn't bear to throw anything away, even cigarette packets. So I *knew* he'd keep the letters, and I knew he'd read them, and re-read them.

(*Slyly.*) And I was crafty, oh I was crafty. I wrote up and down the margins, all over, everywhere! That way he couldn't make them his own by drawing in the margins; that way, they were Kokhlovas, not Picassos!! And that way, sooner or later, those piss-artist critics would have to read what I said.

Clever, eh?

(*A beat.*) I needled the libidinous dwarf. He was only five foot two you know. I was taller than him. Almost anyone was taller than him!

'You haven't got it anymore Pablo,' I'd crow. 'Your son doesn't amount to much either and he's going from bad to worse, like you!'

I'd enclose a photograph, of Beethoven, or Delacroix, or Goya or – just to give him that little extra prod – of Rembrandt, and I'd write on the back: 'If you were like him, *then* you'd be a great artist'.

(*Mussorgsky's Pictures from an Exhibition (No 10.) Piano version.*)
(*Pleasurably.*) If you're going to hurt, do the job properly! One thing about Pablo though, he could recognise quality, but only if he could steal it. Make it his own.

(*With an edge.*) When Paulo was born, it was a new toy, a novelty: it couldn't answer back and it didn't charge for posing.

And it was his. So he used it: lots and lots of lovely drawings.

On each birthday he painted him – until he was four. End of usefulness.

When the boy was eight he painted Paulo as Pierrot.
'Oh the tenderness', 'Oh the affection,' gushed the critics.
Silly bastards!
When did Pablo ever show affection? He'd rise late in
the morning, work until late at night. He couldn't stand
babies crying, and he didn't want to know – unless there
was a photographer present.
Affection? Hah! He'd all the affection of a buzzsaw in a
Siberian forest.

(*Bluntly, and with satisfaction.*) I walked out on the bastard
in 1935. But divorce? Oh nono nonono nonono nono.
Up he comes and tells me, proud as a peacock: I've got a
baby on the way. Well, says I, looking at my flat tummy, and
smiling sweetly at him: which little strumpet is it this time?
(*Innocently.*) Do you realise, if you were to take his penis,
dip it in white paint, and do a modest four inches for
every time he strayed, the line would stretch from Paris
to Monte Carlo!
(*Dryly.*) Wasn't very good in bed mind you. Oh, he had a
great time himself.
That was the problem. He wasn't interested in anybody else.

(*With grim pleasure.*) I walked out on him, oh yes!,
with Paulo!
Went around the corner to the Hôtel California in the
Rue de Berri. He wanted to negotiate.
Negotiate? Him? Hah!
So far as Pablo was concerned, negotiation meant total
agreement: with him! (*Enjoying it.*) So I sent in the
lawyers who sent in the bailiffs to apprise contents, and
then they put seals on the doors of the P Word's studio,
just in case he tried to remove any of the paintings
before a settlement was reached.
(*A beat.*) He exploded. It was delicious!
(*'Listen to this' style.*) At the hearing to determine the
division of property his lawyers tried to make it look as
if I were violent. Didn't I throw dishes... valuable vases,
at him!

Well now, your husband comes home and says, Good afternoon dear, I've been stuffing my penis up some strumpet for the past few years dear. You don't mind, do you dear? Let's have a nice divorce dear. What do you think you'd do? Hand him a cress sandwich and a cucumber? I didn't throw *valuable* vases at him, as a matter of fact: after all, weren't they valuable?

(*Reasonably.*) When we were married I did what papa had always told me to do. I ensured that Pablo signed a community-property agreement which specified that we would share all assets in the event of a divorce. Why ruin valuable china?

(*A beat.*) I threw a chair instead. It was one Pablo bought. Bad taste as usual. He couldn't decorate to save his life.

(*Confidentially.*) Misia Sert was at the hearing. She was, as you will recall, the friend of Mallarmé, Lautrec, Renoir, Bonnard, Vuillard, Diaghilev and – Kokhlova!

(*Slyly.*) Pablo liked her. (*With satisfaction.*) She testified for me!

Pablo got our house in Paris, his paintings, and a bad temper. I got the chateau at Boisgeloup, a handsome allowance, and custody of Paulo.

(*Bortnyansky's Song of the Cherubim.*)

Paulo... poor Paulo... what do you do if you live in the shadow of a shit like Pablo? (*As if Paulo. A whining insistence.*) Papa, pay attention papa, I've no talent papa, help me papa...

(*Amazed.*) So the P Word makes him his chauffeur... his dogsbody...

(*A beat.*) Paulo loved cars. When he was fourteen he had posters of racing drivers on the wall and he crouched on the floor going vroom-vroom with his toy cars.

Once, when I was dying, he went to a *corrida* with Pablo. Cocteau and Prévert, the Picasso gang, they were all there. So Paulo turns up with a friend, Pierre Baudouin, nice boy. From back to front they had shaved exactly one half of their heads. And they were dressed in women's clothes.

Pablo? He contrived not to notice.
(*End music.*)
(*Dryly.*) Pablo always had to be the centre of attention.
And his cronies, the art dealers, the critics, the
journalists, the writers, all basking in the glow of his
fame, all competing for one of his smiles, all crawling
for one of his brushstrokes, all of them, flattering,
fluttering, bending over, simpering like adult children,
sponging for a gift, treating his every word as if came
from Tolstoy or Pushkin... poor Paulo...

(*Elegiacally.*) When I was pregnant with him, the world
changed. The P Word drew those huge mothers with
their huge children...
Amazons... Not like my pretty, elegant portraits.
When we first met he painted me, sitting on an armchair
whose tapestry was ripe and rich with flowers and grapes,
like a Roman Triumph. I had a flowered dress and a
lovely fan...
(*Her tone darkens.*) Before long the harpies came, the
monsters, shrieking onto his sketchbooks and ravening
into his canvas.

You see, he didn't really like change.
Oh, I know what you're thinking. There she goes again.
Such a *silly* woman. Doesn't she know that this man, this
matador of painting, changed the visual world, and
again, and again!
(*'So what' tone.*) Maybe he did. But when I was swelling
with Paulo, he hated it! When Paulo was demanding
attention, he hated it! Because he wanted it! He wanted
routine. He wanted me to stay the same, to be as I was
when we first met. He never grew up and he didn't like
it when I did...

Oh I tried, I tried so hard. Hadn't I been so slim,
so supple... I could slip into any position he wanted.
I wanted my body back, my ballet body, and slowly,

surely as I practised my exercises, it came, it came,
it came!
(*A beat.*) But his eyes were elsewhere. I wasn't *in* his
pictures anymore. Oh. I knew the way his body worked.
That glint in his eye, that charming smile, that throaty
laugh, and whomever he should meet, a schoolgirl on the
street, a friend's wife, a casual encounter in a warm cafe,
his wrist would flex and his mind would start to draw
until he *had* her, naked, legs apart, until the bull would
thrust and gore her, then inseminate.
Submission.

(*Russian Liturgical chant. Or perhaps the Georgian folksong:
Mirangula. Rustavi Choir, St. Petersburg Classics.*)
(*Determined.*) I wouldn't let him, until the honeymoon...
(*With the sheen of reminiscence.*) We were married on the
12th of July, 1918 in the cathedral of Saint Alexander
Nevsky, in Paris. The tapers glittered and gleamed. The
walls were thick with flowers, and the incense shimmered
on the sugared air. The choir were singing...
Taking turns, Cocteau, Max Jacob and Apollinaire held
golden crowns over our heads as we circled the altar,
three times...

> Our marriages are children
> Of this war and triumphant

wrote Apollinaire... but he was wrong...

(*Briskly and sportively.*) We left for Biarritz, a mirage of
baroque and Byzantine palaces, of piney woods near the
lakes; and of *Mimoseraie*, the villa of Madame Eugenia
Errazuriz who had invited us to stay.
Pablo was most attentive, *sportif,* and our bedroom walls,
in between the tumble of tangled limbs with only a ballet
tutu between us, were ripening with the rosy visions of
nude girls who were playing, swimming and dancing.
(*A beat.*) It was long before I realised that he had slid
between *her* legs, maybe even in our bed, and who knows,
maybe even on our honeymoon.

(*Her veneer cracks a little.*)

Oh Pablo... you pursued *me*. What did I do to deserve you?
I did what I knew *how* to do...

(*In a rush.*) We met the best people, I furnished our house
in the best taste, I dressed you properly in a well-cut suit
with a butterfly tie and a gold watch-chain. I gave smart
lunches for the best of society, the Vicomte de Noailles,
Count Étienne de Beaumont; we dined at Giardino's,
we went to balls with Stravinsky and Cocteau and rich
important dealers like the Rosenbergs.

They became your buyers Pablo: you took my world
Pablo; then you spat me out... like an orange pip...

(*Tchaikovsky. <u>Serenade for String Sonata in C Major</u>, Op.48. Pezzo
in forma di Sonatina.*)

When I was twenty-one, against papa's advice, I left
home. Left the Steppes and the silver birch forests.
I wanted to devote myself to dancing.
I had started too late. I knew. Papa knew. But I needed to
prove myself.
And I did.
I joined the dragon Diaghilev. (*Giggles.*) Chinchilla!
Because he had a white lock amidst his dark dyed hair!
(*With delight.*) Oh I worked. *Corps de Ballet*, Monte
Carlo, Roma, Paris, South America. I watched Pavlova
and Karsavina and learnt. I worked and danced with
Nijinsky in *L'Après-midi d'un faune* in a long pleated
tunic of white muslin, stencilled in stripes and leaves of
rust-red.

With Mimi Ramberg who helped us to analyse our roles,
we worked on *The Rite of Spring* with its strange music
which didn't keep to the beat. I was dancing in *Las
Meninas*, was one of the four featured roles in *Les Femmes
de Bonne Humeur.*
I sweated.

Every day, nine o'clock, in white tutu and pink silk tights
for Maestro Cecchetti's class, then change to a *crêpe de
Chine* dress for rehearsal with the régisseur Serge
Grigoriev. I sweated.

Perhaps Diaghilev himself, and friends, would come in.
I sweated. *I made myself.*
I was a featured ballerina! In Diaghilev's company. I had
admirers, across the world. If I wanted men, I could have
men, men of proper social standing, men with a title and
a bank balance, but all I wanted... was the ballet... until
he came...

(*Controlling the emotion.*) Rome, two hotels, and we walked
across the city of moonlight, shadows and fountains.
He drew on menus, napkins, Chinchilla's ivory walking
stick!
'No, no Monsieur Picasso,' I'd say as he'd scrape his
knuckles on my door at the end of the night. And in the
evening light, after dinner, as Cocteau was wooing the
Chinchilla with lipstick and rouge, he'd start to sketch
me and I'd tell him, 'I want to recognise my face
Monsieur Picasso. My face. Not your self!' And
he'd laugh.
And in the morning he'd look puzzled. 'Why you
breaking your shoe in door?'
To soften the point, Monsieur. 'Pablo,' he'd say, 'if you
won't go to bed, at least call me Pablo!'

When I called him Pablo, there was Revolution in
Russia. The Tzar abdicated.
Papa was ruined.
We went to Barcelona to meet his *maman*. 'I don't believe
any woman could be happy with my son. He's only
available for himself.'
Hah! I thought. Old witch.
He was frightened of her. She knew too much...

1954. I was dying. Was it worth it? Hah!
Paulo had just had a hernia operation, then a lung
embolism. The surgeon sent a telegram to Pablo, urging
him to visit.
He didn't.
I was partially paralysed. Cancer diagnosed.

I wondered if he'd visit.

He didn't.

January. Paulo was still in hospital, in Paris. In Cannes, I lay in my hospital bed. White walls, just like the first house that I decorated for you, Pablo... clean, tidy, organised.

I took a turn for the worse.

I wanted to be buried in the Russian Orthodox church in Cannes. They buried me at Vallauris. There were three people at the funeral.

Pablo didn't come.

(*She begins to laugh.*)

(*Then gently.*) Порá éхатъ спокóйной нóчи (It's time to go. Goodnight.)

But don't worry Pablo, up here you can't escape.

I'll find you, you little pipsqueak bastard. I'll find you, if I have to brave the Gates of Hell itself. I'll find you and I'll watch you, roasting slowly, tormented by naked nubile angels, unable to get it up Pablo, a failure for all eternity Pablo, a piss-artist who can't *paint* Pablo, a waste of space... (*She gives a victorious whoop.*)

(*Return to Shostakovich's Twelfth.*)

The End.

MARIE-THÉRÈSE

The fiction of the monologue is that Marie-Thérèse is dead but currently inhabiting the body that she died with. She can recall any element of her past but she does so with the thoughts and feelings of that particular moment.

Contrary to much received (male) opinion, my Marie-Thérèse is a gentle, likeable woman who always wants to think the best of everyone. Her voice has infinite gradations of tenderness, wistfulness, warmth and nostalgic longing.

In terms of music, the possibilities are Debussy, Dukas (e.g. The Sorcerer's Apprentice, which could almost be a metaphor for her relationship with Picasso), Fauré, Milhaud, Ravel, Satie and Poulenc. I'd suggest that the bright cheerful quality of Poulenc is the logical one, especially as the melancholy beauty of the adagietto from Les Biches would make an excellent coda at the end of the piece. But Milhaud is another strong contender in that the sensual world of La Création du Monde suggests the constant analogies between Marie-Thérèse and the natural world, which Picasso made in his paintings.

Each dramatic monologue is a bit like the overlapping facet or perspective in a cubist painting. Incidents, motifs, and versions of events appear and re-appear.

Darkness. The room we will be observing, the stage room that is, is a flat in Boulevard Henri-Quatre in 1944. This is the room which still exists in the imaginative recreation of Marie-Thérèse Walter. Whether we see it or not, depends on the director. Perhaps it is simply an empty space, except for the rear of the stage which is covered with either reproductions (or projected slides) of those works which Picasso made of Marie-Thérèse Walter during the thirties. We start with the opening glissando from Debussy's Jeux which suggests grace, dexterity and movement.

~

Fade in and up, the sounds of a trim young woman exercising on the trampoline. As the lights rise, the trampoline sounds fade, and she glides in, an ethereal vision made manifest.

MARIE-THÉRÈSE: They'll tell you he stopped loving me.
  It's not true! Really! Cross my heart and hope to die.
  (*Giggles. Her infectious silvery giggles run like a leitmotif though her speech.*)
  I am a ninny! How can I hope to die when I'm dead already?
  (*Wistfully.*) No need of a trampoline now...
  But just look at me! Thirty-four years old, blonde, tall,

shapely, *pneumatique* as the boys used to say. Well actually they used to say things that were much ruder than that!

Tristan, Tristan Tzara that is, you know! That nice Romanian boy with a mouth like a sewer who used to write poetry that I never could understand, well he said that if you gave me a good novelette and a box of chocolates, then I could be... you know... (*She doesn't wish to offend by saying 'fucked'.*) ... without being distracted... but that was only because I wouldn't sleep with him.
He couldn't believe that I wouldn't sleep with him, but he was a nice man because he told Pablo that what Pablo needed was a blonde, and then Pablo found me!

Oh dear! I really am a ninny! Here I am, chattering on as we look at me in 1944.
(*Brightly: too brightly.*) *Why* does that year matter?

(*A loving tone: imitates Picasso's thick accent.*)
'Today Marie-Thérèse, the 13th of July 1944, is the seventeenth anniversary of your birth in me, and also your own birth into this world where, having met you, I have begun to live.'
(*With gentle certainty.*) D'you think he ever wrote such lovely words to Olga, or Dora or Françoise?

July 13, 1937, my birthday.
I was eighteen, and we went to a hotel in Neuilly.
(*Giggles.*) But I haven't told you how we met!
It was six months earlier, a cold day in January and I was standing in front of the Galeries Lafayette department store on the Boulevard Haussmann, waiting on a girlfriend. And there he was in his fine thick overcoat, staring at me. He even walked around me once or twice as if he couldn't believe his eyes.
(*She imitates his thick accent again.*)
'Miss. You have an interesting face. I would like to do your portrait. I am Picasso.'
Well *I* didn't know who he was, did I? That took him

by surprise! He looked as if he couldn't *quite* believe it. But I wasn't interested in paintings.

(*A hint of Satie creeps in.*)
Did I tell you that my father was a painter? No?
I never met my daddy. On my birth certificate it says 'Father unknown'.
Mummy liked paintings, and she played classical music on the piano and read classical literature but I never bothered with any of that. Now gymnastics, that I do enjoy – but I'm forgetting, aren't I!

He simply grabbed me by the arm and asked if I'd like breakfast.
I was hungry, and it was free so I had a plate of bacon and eggs, a whole basket of rolls, and four cups of coffee.
Well, what use is a croissant to a gymnast?
(*The Satie fades...*)
And he was so amazed that he asked me if I was English as he'd never seen anyone other than the English or the Americans eating like that so early in the morning.
Poor dear! He was such a... a diabolical man... but I know he couldn't help it.
(*Brightly.*) We met two days later at Saint-Lazare metro.
(*Giggles. Imitates his accent.*)
'We will do great things together.'
I'm afraid to say that I burst out laughing!

But wasn't he a foreigner, and a nice man, with a lovely thick accent like treacle.
He was wearing a blue serge suit, but he never could keep the creases. He always had things in his pockets, packets of cigarettes, small sketch books, matches, bits of crayon, pencils.
(*An odd piquant tone.*) And he had a white shirt with a red-and-black tie.
(*Brightly.*) I still have the tie!

(*A touch of Poulenc's Voyage à Paris with its echoes of Maurice Chevalier.*)

And when he'd shove his hands into his coat pockets, searching for something, the tips of the fingers would be grubby with crayon dust and bits of tobacco.

He told me he was married but I didn't care. He had such beautiful blackcurrant eyes, and a thick, dark, shiny lock of hair that wandered over his forehead. And he was so... so stocky, proud, erect, he seemed to look at you and into you and all around you, and will you to do what he wanted and he had such powerful yet feminine hands.

You've understood me, haven't you?

A woman doesn't resist Picasso.

I did for six months. I was seventeen.

I knew nothing. I was innocent, a gamine, but it was *me* that he selected, me, out of the hundreds, the thousands who threw themselves at him.

(*The Poulenc gradually fades.*)

Did you know that Manet did the same? It's true. Pablo told me. Manet was strolling along the boulevards when he saw Victorine Meurant amongst the crowds and *he selected her* and she became his model and his inspiration and she lives now in his paintings.

You remember that one, *The Picnic.* Doesn't she look beautiful? And it's her you look at because everyone else has their clothes on!

(*A beat.*) I never really thought of him as 'old'.

I suppose he would have been older than my father, whoever he was, because Pablo must have been, oh, forty-six or forty-seven, but he didn't make you think of age...

We used to go to suburban bars and discreet hotels, even boating on the Mearne, though he always said that he hated water.

(*A touch of Milhaud's La Création du Monde.*)

Once I stayed at a children's camp while Picasso and Olga stayed nearby. We had to be very careful because I was legally a minor and the French law took 'the corruption of a minor' very seriously.

But he could be so terribly gentle. He asked me, right at
the start, if I would help him with his fantasies.
(*With élan.*) What did I know of how to please a man?
He taught me. (*Giggles.*) I only know what he was
kind enough to show me and I've never wanted any
other man.
At first I used to laugh at what he wanted. Well, if you're
seventeen or eighteen, it's a giggle, isn't it? He didn't
want me to laugh though. He was always telling me to
be serious. Poor Pablo. He needed so much, and so often,
and in such funny positions.
(*A beat.*) I didn't always like the... the sore bits... but it
was an adventure, wasn't it?
(*Convincing herself.*) It was an adventure!

Did you know that he wrote poetry about me? I was the
only one who touched him to words.
(*A beat. She produces a much-worn sheaf of paper.*)
'A slice of melon which never remains quiet, laughing at
everything as long as summer lasts, a lilac dove, a
laughing mare'.
He didn't want people to know. It was our secret, so he
used to write in his little black sketchbooks that he
carried in his pocket and if he couldn't think of the right
word he'd put in a tiny blob of colour and then later he'd
do little line drawings around them.
(*In a rush.*) And he would always write me letters in the
later years, lovely letters, each of them starting with our
monogram, MTW looped into P, and each of them
ending with the date in roman numerals.
(*The Milhaud fades...*)
And he'd write, and I'd hear him in my head...
(*Imitates his voice.*)
'I love you a bit more every instant... beautiful love of
my life... Marie-Thérèse of my heart'...
They're honest words, aren't they?
And there'd be little sketches around the edges,
of bouquets of rampant flowers, of me... rampant!

I always cried with Pablo. I bowed my head in front of him. He was so, so wonderfully terrible. And he used to tell me stories.

(*Brightly.*) There was the one about two lovers, one French, one Spanish, who lived together happily and lovingly until she learnt to speak his language, and then he noticed how stupid she was – so the romance was at an end.

It was such a sad, sad story, and I know Olga made him very unhappy. He said I banished the monsters from his paintings whereas she put them in!

Of course he kept making paintings and drawings.
(*She looks at the images on the walls.*)
I must admit that they didn't really bowl me over. I kept telling him when he started to paint me all the time. 'But they don't look like me Pablo!'

And he'd smile and say 'But they don't have to Marie-Thérèse. A painting is not a reflection. It's a jaw that snatches at a bit of the soul!'
(*The Satie begins to creep in again...*)
(*Brightly.*) So Pablo had his painting and I had my cycling, my mountaineering, my table-tennis and my gymnastics.
(*A beat.*) Sometimes he used to ask me if I'd like to go to a *vernissage* so I would ask him if he'd like to go mountaineering!

Oh, he was so, so various a man. There was always something else happening.

When he bought Boisgeloup it was like visiting this new world, a chateau with a park and stables and outhouses of all sorts like a coach-house and a great round dovecot and a lovely Gothic chapel in the courtyard, facing the stables, which he turned into studios and started to people with sculptures, only nobody knew for, oh, years and years and years, that they were all of *me*!

There was no electricity, just the kerosene lamps, and the junk – the bolts and the pots and pans, the car fenders, the twisted hoods, the wood and the plaster, the cardboard,

and the palm fronds beachcombed from the strands,
the tins and the worn-out wicker baskets, the broken jugs
and the springs underfoot, and the bits of wire sticking out
in all directions invaded by the stacks of cigarette cartons
and the towers of matchboxes, and me and me and me and
me, huge heads in plaster rising out of the junk seas and
gleaming whitely in the dark shadows, and on a warm day
we'd lie in each other's arms, naked, looking at me and me
and me, and he'd want to explore and he'd tell me that only
someone who had the right key could open my body like a
wardrobe, and he would and only he had the key, and when
I was unlocked his hand would reach out, and whatever it
touched, whether it was a splay of wire or a flange of
cardboard, his fingers would bend and twist and shape and
turn and a piece of junk would birth and a baby sculpture
would slide out of the shadows to play upon my breast or
perch upon my shoulder. (*A beat.*) One late late afternoon as
his fingers slid from shoulder to wire, the tilly lamp threw
its shadow on the wall. He became erect, excited,
galvanised, his eyes gleaming in the dark as he scrabbled to
his feet and in no time he was adding plaster. He had seen
me on the wall he said, and he must have done, because
when Olga saw the sculpture, it intrigued her he said.
Something was different. It didn't seem invented.
(*With elation.*) So she sulked!

(*Satie. From* Parade.)
I can't honestly say that I liked such modern works. He took
all the bits of my face and re-arranged them, and did things
to them, so that a nose became like a huge penis, or a mouth
became a vulva but I suppose he knew what he was doing
because as I found out much later, an awful lot of people
wanted to buy them so I suppose they must be good.
He would say...
(*Imitates his voice.*)
'To displace. To contradict. To show one eye full-face and
one in profile.
Nature does many things the way I do but she hides
them! My painting is a series of cock-and-bull stories!'

But you see I never really cared for the idea of the famous painter. I wanted him for *me*, not for the world. I just liked to be *with* him.

And I had to lie more and more to mummy, saying I was spending the afternoon with a girlfriend.

(*A beat.*) But I think she knew... didn't a painter give her me?

Pablo told me that Olga discovered *me* in his pictures at the Galerie Georges Petit.

He told me what Tristan said.

(*She imitates the Romanian.*)

'If she tries to tackle Marie-Thérèse with her handbag and abuse, her skull, with its tiny brain, will be cracked between those two huge and perfectly formed thighs, like a lemon in a nutcracker'.

I think he was very rude to call my thighs 'huge'.

(*Satie begins to fade...*)

I had to have an abortion. He didn't want a baby then. And mama agreed, so when I was swimming I just... stopped. He was somewhere at the edge of the pool and it was a while before he or anyone else realised.

Of course I said I'd had a cramp. He was so nice to me, so kind, I was his poor Ophelia nearly drowned in a cup of water, and when I asked him who Ophelia was, he told me of this painting of a beautiful lady, floating down a stream...

(*Milhaud snakes back in...*)

It was just over two years later that we had the baby.

(*With perfect Spanish pronunciation, enjoying the sounds.*)

We'd gone to Spain in the hot Summer, from Irun to San Sebastian, from Burgos to Madrid...

... el Escorial, Toledo and Zaragoza... through Aragón, and then home to Barcelona; and not a journalist had so much as caught sight of me!

October the fifth; the Belvedere clinic in Boulogne.

I didn't know it then, but when Maya was being born he

was window-shopping for a new lady friend; Dora as
it happened.
It was just that he always needed someone new, but he
never stopped loving me. Never!
I called her Maria de la Concepción, after Pablo's
little sister who died at the age of four in La Coruña.
Pablo and my half sister went to the city hall to register
her birth...
... 'father unknown'...
(*Musically, associate this 'father unknown' with that of her own*
'father unknown' earlier in the script.)
(*In a rush.*) What else could he do and he being married
to Olga and he telling me that he'd ask for a divorce?
And he did, but then the war in Spain broke out and the
Nationalists forbade divorce to any Spanish subject...

She looked so like him, did Maya; had the same stocky
shoulders, the same broad face; and she was so so pretty.
He bought a house for us on the Riviera, at Juan-les-Pins,
and for two whole months we had him to ourselves. So
much planning he had to do, the poor dear!

He wrote to me in Paris, reminding me to bring the sheets
and to turn off the gas, the electricity and the water.
(*Produces sheaf of paper again.*)
'I love you still more than yesterday and less than
tomorrow. I will always love you as they say – I love
you (*She starts to imitate his accent.*) I love you I love you
I love you Marie-Thérèse.'
And he did!

While I breast-fed Maya, swam, and furnished the house
and breast-fed Maya again, he went to Cannes to look at the
boats in the harbour. And we stayed in bed until ten in the
morning, our little honeymoon, and he sang to Maya, and
he sketched and he painted and I even got him to write
letters to Sabartés his secretary and to Tristan.
(*With pride.*) He washed nappies for me and...
(*An edge of black emotion nearly obtrudes.*)

... nearly thirty years later I was looking at the pictures in a book, pictures of works that Pablo had done at this time which had never been seen before. And there I was, dead, my naked body being carried away by two nude women, and one of them had the dark wavy hair of Dora Maar.

But that's just my imagination, isn't it?
We all have nightmares. It's just that Pablo paints his.

(*Brightly.*) During the war I moved back to Paris, Boulevard Henri-Quatre. Pablo had a studio on the Rue des Grands-Augustins.
Dora of course liked to think of herself as his official mistress but she never realised, none of them did, that they were only there for a few short years, whereas I was there for ever.
(*In confidence.*) You see, there were two spiral staircases up to his studio.
Poor Sabartés always thought that he used one for Dora, and one for me, but he was quite forgetful at times!

One afternoon I went into him.
'You've been promising to marry me for so long,' I said, 'and now it's about time that you did!'
And do you know what he said?
Imitates his voice.
'At my age Marie-Thérèse, you know, it would be a little ridiculous. Besides there's a war on, that makes matters complicated –'
And just at that point, in arrives Dora, listening behind the door no doubt!

(*Imitates her voice.*)
'Look Pablo, you're in love with me, and you know it!'
And do you know what he did? He put his arm around me, *me*, and he said:
(*Imitates his voice.*)
'Dora Maar, you know perfectly well that the only woman I love is Marie-Thérèse Walter, and that's that!'

But would she leave? I had to take her by the scruff of
the shoulders and push her out the door!
(*Imitates Picasso's voice.*)
'You know how much I love you!'
And I do! (*A beat.*) Then he gave me my five kilos of
coal. Every day he did, to keep me and Maya warm. And
he opened a big wardrobe.
(*Imitates his voice.*)
'You see that gold. If anything happens to me, it's yours!'
He always was a hoarder, was Pablo. But I was looking
at the two towers of good yellow soap. I'd rather have
the soap now, I said, but he just smiled and closed
the door.

He always loved Maya. I know he did. Sketchbook after
sketchbook he filled... Maya sleeping... Maya smiling...
Maya growing up. He would even try to feed her when
she was a baby.
(*Imitates his voice.*)
'A child who doesn't eat, dies!' he would say.
When she was twenty he sent her to Cartier's to pick out
whatever she wanted. And she did, but her father never
sent the money along, so she had to do without.
I suppose he must have forgotten...
There was only once when I was frightened. In 1969.
Of course he was married to that woman then, that
Jacqueline. And the payments stopped.
What was I to do? I had no other money... so I wrote
him a letter, didn't sign it. (*A beat.*)
In the first year that we met he did a painting, *Composition
with Letters and White Hand*. He always kept it with him.
Our monogram is on the hand... so I wrote:

> 'I say that the hand is frightening, the hand raised
> for false oaths, the hand that clutches the rifle, the
> hand that braids the barbed wire, the hand that
> strikes, the hand that kills. I say that the hand is
> wretched, the wounded hand, the hand that begs,
> the hand that forgets, the hand in chains, in
> despair, the hand of death.'

He never wrote back.

Maya found an art dealer for me who came over from America. I didn't want to sell my Picassos, but what else could I do? I had Maya to think of.

When he came I showed him all my letters.

It was cold.

And my little packages wrapped in tissue.

I used to clip his fingernails...

And he went away and he saw Pablo and he asked him to sign the pictures so that I could sell them. Pablo said he would but then Jacqueline came in. The pictures belonged to Pablo! Never would he sign them!

I knew what she was at and so I went to the lawyer's, and of course he fulfilled his 'natural obligations' under French law as I knew he always would.

Such a short time he had then...

When he died I went to his house at Vauvenargues but they wouldn't let me in. A gendarme and a gardener came out to tell me that they were suffering so much inside the chateau that they couldn't receive me.

We weren't even allowed to go to the funeral, not me or Maya or Claude or Paloma... or Pablito.

Just a few days before, Pablo had written to me. April the first.

(*Produces the letter.*)

'You were the only woman I ever loved.'

(*Brightly.*) Paulo, Pablo's son, told Pablito that Jacqueline refused to allow him to go to his grandfather's funeral. So on the morning of the funeral Pablito drank a container of potassium chloride bleach. When they got him to hospital it was too late to save his digestive organs.

He had no money, so I ended up selling some of my Picassos after all, to pay for the operations. I couldn't see him suffer, could I?... but he died.

(*Fade in the melancholy beauty of the adagietto of Poulenc's Les Biches.*)

It was an irresistible compulsion. He loved me. I loved him. Someone had to look after him, someone had to follow him. He was my Pablo.

So I went down to Juan-les-Pins, where we had our 'little honeymoon', and I was happy as I went into the garage.

(*Brightly.*) It's handy, having been a gymnast I mean. I knew all about weights and balance. As I threw the rope over the beam in the garage, it was as if he was drawing the line in space as it snaked over the beam. I could see his pencil knot it neatly in one continuous line, careful not to bruise my neck.

The lights slowly fade until the only thing we can see is her face, and, on the back wall, a painting of the splayed-legged voluptuousness of the erstwhile MARIE-THÉRÈSE.

I jumped Pablo, hoping to find your arms, and I will, I know I will, because you're here, somewhere in this vast and echoing eternity, and I'll search Pablo, you know I will, I'll search and I'll search Pablo, I'll search until I find you... Pablo... my love...

Then the light fades on MARIE-THÉRÈSE's face. And finally, it also fades out on the image of herself in the painting.

The End.

DORA

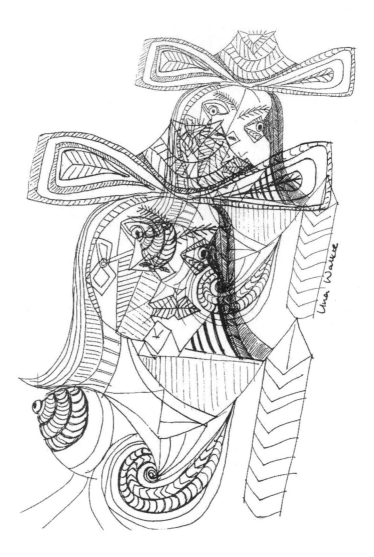

Everyone is agreed: Dora Maar had a remarkable voice. Her friend James Lord referred to the 'extraordinary birdsong resonance of her intonations'. She was extremely intelligent, one of the 'bluestockings' of the Surrealist movement: thus the voice should mirror her qualities: alert, perceptive, often dryly witty.

She was born in the provinces of France, spent her formative childhood years in Argentina before being domiciled in Paris, and could speak Spanish, French and Serbo-Croat fluently – her father being Serbo-Croat, her mother French.

My Dora exists, for the purposes of the play, on two levels. Her monologue gives us access to the early Dora, a sceptical, iconoclastic, free-wheeling spirit: independently minded. And the convention is that this Dora can confront or reflect upon her present-tense life. The other Dora however is the image of herself that Picasso constructed, and which she eventually became: compliant; doormat; hermit.

I suggest that the music of Les Six might stitch together the markedly contrasting elements of Dora's story and personality. I've also felt quite free to suggest a contrapuntal element to all this (Stravinsky, Varèse et al), not to mention the dotting of some genetic elements (Argentinian and Serbian references), as Dora is not a linear construction. But although there are a range of specific suggestions in the text, they should not be taken as prescriptive.

Between the late thirties and the mid forties, Picasso did a remarkable series of portraits of Dora. She became, for him, 'the weeping woman' and critics have interpreted this as her becoming a symbol of the social and political angst of the period. Frankly it is more likely that she was revealing the tormented nature of her psyche – at the hands of Picasso. Images of this period, whether in terms of cut-outs flown down, back projections, or motifs freely used by a designer, would make an admirable set. Another possibility is to use Guernica or sections of it (for Dora is there) as a backdrop.

~

A splay of South American rhythms, syncopated to splays of light, illuminating images from the set, which builds rapidly to a climax – cut on a diminuendo of dry, snake-rattle percussion. Silence. A few more, half-hearted, snake-rattles on the percussion, before the gradual onset of light reveals DORA to us.

DORA: I am not dead yet, but I know that I have died.
And no, I do not need your help, do not require your help, do not desire your help.
I am my own construction: was my own construction.
I will be... inviolate...

(*Stravinsky's* Rite of Spring *with its pounding barbaric chords slides in.*)
Such a neat and unrewarding irony: who cast the horoscope?
Smile!
For I was born in the year of that beautiful barbarity, *Les Demoiselles d'Avignon.* 1907...
... *une fleur du mal...*
A vision, a re-vision, a liberation!
(*Gleefully.*) The subterranean squelches the surface!
(*The music stops sharply.*)

(*Joyously.*) *Merde*!
(*A beat.*)
(*Deflated.*) My story too...
(*Deadpan.*) *Sainte-Anne* in the fourteenth arrondissement.
The psychiatric hospital.
The Madhouse.
I watched as they strapped me in, tied the flaps over my ankles, my calves, my wrists. He knew where I was but *he* didn't come. And then they –
(*Stiffens and jerks as if she has been tied and gagged. The crackle of electricity. She buckles and half screams through the gag. Another crackle of electricity: it seems to go on, and on, and on. She whimpers.*)

Nine long days, but he never came. It was Paul, Paul Éluard, a quiet and gentle man, the poet who introduced me to Picasso...
(*A crackle of electricity. She whimpers and gibbers to herself as the electroshock treatment continues: a brief collage of different voltages – the underlying buzz and crackle varying in pitch and sonority –*

*heard against the gibbering in which we catch her repeated words
'God' (now pleading, now a scream) and 'forgive' – this latter
word dying away into silence.)*

(*Assertively.*) ... it was *Paul*, quiet, gentle Paul who rampaged
into Picasso's studio, shattered a chair and *demanded* that the
minotaur come out of hiding.

(*Dismissively.*) He never could stand illness, could Picasso.
Un Malagueño malagradecido (The ungrateful Malagan.)
(*With quiet venom.*) For that superstitious, irreligious
Spaniard, it was the mark of death, waiting to claw into
him. ¡*Bastardo* ! *Con los hombres nunca se sabe...* (With men
you never know.)

Does he come?
(*Coolly, yet acerbically.*) Those of you who are thinking
'Yes' should be removed to the Madhouse. I have no time
for fools... (*Softly.*) Even handsome fools.
No, he sends for his personal physician. (*Scornfully.*) Oh yes,
our great and glorious monarch of twentieth-century art
had his own tame doctor, a psychoanalyst no less, one
Jacques Lacan, whom he summoned even for a common
cold but paid with the gold of a quick sketch.

(*Deadpan.*) Into analysis and the private clinic... And
when I emerged? (*A short harsh laugh.*) I was made into
someone that I soon became...
(*Teasingly.*) But I anticipate.
Who's there?
(*With largesse.*) Ah, splendid... Show in the infinite...
(*Starts to laugh.*) All of his women got shock treatment...

(*Milhaud. A jazzy riff with sparkling piano and trombones.*)
(*With brisk good humour.*) Picasso? No such thing. Pic-cass-oes!
He, they, changed more than his, and their, spots!
You want to know what a Picasso is?
Of course you do. Everybody does.

Cross a randy goat with an instinct for Art, patch in a penis which paints, opening the legs of under-aged schoolgirls, smart tarts going under the soubriquet of reporters, and virginal wives; add fame and serious fortune and the promise of immortality, and who would not succumb?

(*A beat.*) *We all did, undressing for his pencil, splaying our limbs for his quick tongue, opening an orifice for the five-finger exercise of his brush.*

(*Music ends sharply.*)

What *is* a Picasso? You wish to know? He's the place where he lived, stacked and cluttered, littered and scumbled, made manifest in his own image.

(*Sourly.*) He's the dog of the day, whether mongrel or Afghan, feted and fawned upon, then dumped when it's hooked.

He's the sinewy poet who served as a catalyst, cast off when the artist gets bored – as he will...

He's the circle of friends, (*With cutting aplomb.*) arselickers and arseholes, who drench him admiringly, with understanding and praise.

He's the woman with whom he *claimed* to be in love, who came when he whistled, her arse in the air...

(*Satie's Parade.*)

(*Deadpan.*) Nice man... Picasso... we bent to his will...

(*Irritably.*) Oh, it wasn't just the sex. Wasn't I more than usually well-informed in respect of that discipline! Take Georges... I did!

(*Briskly.*) He was married to a sweetly pretty actress called Sylvia, nice little daughter, splendidly handsome house. When I first met him he was in the cellar, rooting around amidst a Babel of pornography, joyfully brandishing this and that like a truffle hunter, obsessed with writing his novels on the philosophy of carnal desire; a connoisseur who believed in transgressing all sexual limitations.

(*End music.*)

He had an admirable pedigree, did Georges Bataille,
literary lion, member of the Surrealists, a handsome,
charming man. So naturally I became his mistress.
(*With sweet reasonableness.*)
Was not I too a Surrealist, a painter, a photographer, a
collagist? Didn't we all believe in sexual freedom? Why
believe what you don't practise?

(*The Aboriginal music of la Puna (Argentina) – a melody using the
tritone interval, suggesting a pre-Inca culture.*)
I was free! Free from my mother who converted to
Catholicism; free from my architect father who never
succeeded when he could fail; free from my youth
in Argentina.
I started to paint.
I worked with Brassai and Man Ray, exploring the
world of the darkroom, publishing my images in the
little magazines, finding my visual voice as I became
aware that images chose *me*... those dark echoing
tunnels with obscure presences... lurking...
And so I turned to photomontage; and the hands moved
and the scissors snipped of their own accord...
(*In a rush.*) ... the images rose unbidden and I was *accepted*,
elated, the chosen companion of men like Bataille, Brassai,
André Breton, Eluard, Michel Leiris and Man Ray.
I was muse *and* artist, and what a coup it would be if
I should decide to become *maîtresse en titre* to the
acknowledged legislator of the modern world... Picasso.
(*End music.*)

(*Dismissively.*) It was easy. Fawning courtiers galore;
women who poured themselves towards him, so naturally
he lapped a little, then tossed aside. But I would make
him come to me. I was twenty-nine and he was fifty-five.

(*Poulenc's Sonata for Violin and Piano.*)
(*Reminiscing.*) Twenty-nine, 'the madonna without a
smile', I could be seen in Montparnasse at *Le Dôme*,

La Rotonde or *Le Select.*

Man Ray had photographed me: Brassai had photographed
me. I had fine slender hands, tipped with diamond red, and
a body in bloom.

(*Bluntly.*) But I also had a brain!

(*Enjoying herself.*) It was at the *Deux Magots.*

He was sitting across the way, surrounded by the courtiers,
pleased at being the centre of attention.

Everyone kept glancing towards him: so I ignored him.
Then I carefully, and slowly, peeled off my black gloves,
embroidered with little pink flowers, and as he regaled
his audience, I started to seriously play, my fingers
splayed out on the cafe table, my sharp little penknife
poised in the air, and then I stabbed downwards, staccato
tattoo between the fingers, backwards, forwards, nicking
the flesh, faster, slower, a rhythmic beat, the drops of
scarlet pricking my white flesh, rhyming with my
fingernails...

... and as I had anticipated, his voice had tapered ...
into silence.

I looked up: he was staring intently at me. The
garçon had arrived so, with careful absent-mindedness,
I requested (*With the speed and attack of a native.*) *Café
con leche por favor.*

(*Bluntly.*) According to Nush Éluard, wasn't Picasso
always complaining that he had no one to speak to in
Spanish... so... I picked up my gloves and left. One
should always intrigue, don't you think?

(*A touch of ripe Fauré.*)

Naturally, as the minotaur spent summers at Mougins,
I was domiciled there, at Lise Deharmes's, before
he arrived.

(*Reminiscing.*) Imagine a medieval village, on a hill dotted
with olive and cypress, overlooking the bay of Cannes,
fragrant with an undergrowth of cistus and lentisk.

Warm sea breezes, the village *vin rose*. Perfect for a
bricolage of landscape and faces and camera spaces.

(*Amused.*) Lise just happened to be a friend of Paul who
had a flat in the village, and an acquaintance of Picasso
who was staying at the rambling and aptly named *Hôtel
Vaste Horizon*, – wasn't it decorated with the naif canvases
of a local gendarme which were to amuse Picasso greatly?
– so what more natural than a visit from the *malagueño*
himself – Lise was *enchantée et boulversée* at the invitation
to join his party to bathe at the beach the following
morning – though as Paul had anticipated that dirty gypsy
Tristan Tzara was in attendance.

(*A touch of the whirling Kolo, the national dance of the Serbs.*)
'Marcovitch? Isn't that a Serb name? I wouldn't trust a
Serb, not even to murder a Croat!'
But before I could nail his tongue to a passing yardarm,
his mouth dropped open, his swimming trunks bulged –
no self control these Romanians and wasn't the *malagueno*
in the same condition? – and this blonde girl, naked to the
waist, with breasts so solid that you could kill flies with
them, emerges from the waves.
Rose Marie she called herself, all dumb laughter and
athletic golf assurance.

If the minotaur thought that I would condescend to *that*,
he had to be taught otherwise. So I walked off. (*Deadpan.*)
Tzara should be grateful to me: Rose Marie was delivered
into his bed.
(*Dryly.*) As for the minotaurian *malagueño*, some half
hour later as I walked along the beach, it was ¡*Que hubo*!
as he caught my hand, prattled on about the monstrous
Olga who refused to give him a divorce, about his
little daughter Maya, about the lack of intelligent
company – oh it was his dammed-up birthright of
Spanish, cascading out!
(*With hauteur.*) As a French speaker he was incompetent.

Appalling accent, twisted grammar: but why should he
care when everyone hung upon his every word, seeking
complexity where none existed?

(*George Antheil's Ballet Mécanique – 1925.*)
The words skimmed out with the speed of his
pencil. He expected pretty women to be available
and vacuous –
(*With justifiable pride.*) But was brought up short as he
realised that I had studied painting at the *Académie Julien
et L'Académie Passy*, had served my time at *L'École des Arts
Décoratifs*, then become one of the select handful, taken
up by Brassai at *L'École de Photographie*. I earned my
living as a professional photographer and had a painting
that year in the International Surrealist Exhibition at the
New Burlington Galleries, London.
I was *not* a Marie-Thérèse.

Before long he was changing his routine, (*With satisfaction.*)
arising early, taking me for long walks on the beach.
You'll find a drawing of the period. (*With gleeful malice.*)
You know the kind: scholars drool over the archetypal
configurations!
Šta to znači? (*Pronounced 'Shta toh z'nachee'?*)
What does it mean? Simple!
You see a bearded patriarch, with his staff and his dog,
and a young girl dressed for a journey.
Even Lacan could work that out!! An inflated ego. Old
man takes young girl on a journey:
(*Mae West style.*) Come up and see my etchings some time...
His ego, of course, was punctilious in its accuracy. I assumed
that I could, and would control...
(*End music.*)

And yet... (*Reminiscing fondly.*) Bronzed skin, agile...
energy as restless as the tumbling waves...
... at dinner he'd be Charlie Chaplin, hit on the head with
a brick; Hitler with a black toothbrush as a moustache;
Franco or Mussolini...

... on a tablecloth he'd sketch a portrait with a burnt
match, create a sculpture with a napkin and a few corks...
He could make anything *live*!

(*Debussy's La Mer.*)
(*With controlled amusement.*) On the beach he was forever
stopping to stuff a pebble into his pocket, or we would
be picking up a piece of pottery or glass, worn smooth
by the sea. Everything would be pouring down the throat
of his imagination!
We even took to carrying a shopping basket, filling it
with the blanched roots of seaweed or the sea-eaten rafts
of driftwood, that lay beached by the rustling tide.
Within days the stones would be engraved, the wood
and the glass and the pottery would deliver a fecund
sculpture, and the pattern on salt-encrusted stone, the
striation on a ripple of driftwood or the pockmarked
plenty on a shard of pottery would slide onto the page
in a scrake of sketchbook glory.

'*Nužda ne poznaje zakona*' (*Pronounced 'noozhda neh
poz'nayah zahkohma'.*) I told him, remembering a proverb
that daddy was forever telling...
Necessity knows no law.
He learnt it off!!
'*Nužda ne poznaje zakona*', he kept repeating, rubbing his
hands delightedly, smiling and gambolling like a child
on the sand. I should have realised.
(*Dryly.*) Is not genius, in some sense, the capacity for
literalism?
(*Introduce strains of a baroque dance tune, perhaps Lully, Rameau
or Couperin.*)
Before we left for Paris, I cast his horoscope... (*Giggles.*)...
it was almost exactly the same as that of Louis the
Fourteenth! Indomitable energy and perseverance. Pure
despotism!
(*With enormous satisfaction.*) Within a month I had begun
to appear in his painting. He drew me in pen-and-ink

first, quick sketches to cream the surface of appearance
before he quarried in paint.
(*End music.*)
(*With pleasure.*) Once, I am drawn... asleep. Marie-Thérèse
had been the muse of sleep... but now her sleep, her precious
painterly sleep, I have stolen away...
I am muse, *maîtresse en titre,* I am empowered!
What more could I ask? Will I not learn? Will I not grow
in the shade of this eternity-maker?
Surely my work – my art – will flourish with his
encouragement and by his example?
(*Deadpan.*) Each night I return to my parents at the Rue
de Savoie. He is, for a while, a secret in guilt.

(*Varèse's* <u>Ecuatorial</u> (*1934*) *– a Maya incantation with the
thereminsprominent.*)
(*Gently, but with an unsettling edge.*) And then I find, here
and there in the studio, oh so carelessly disarrayed, letters
from her, Marie-Thérèse; and as we go to lunch, he has
a letter to post and I glimpse, ever ever so accidentally,
her name.
And as a year passes he slithers his scorn in a thousand
quips on sterile women. And oh how beautiful is little
Maya! How like her father! How like her mother!
Her fecund mother...

And nothing comes, nothing grows, nothing burgeons
in this womb of mine. And I feel the failure in this
burgeoning world of rampant canvas, and quicksilver
paper; where a bent nail, a handlebar and a bicycle
saddle can birth into a bull's head!
I fight him! I can be temper-tantrum too!
(*End music.*)

(*As a serious question.*) Am I depressed?
(*A beat.*)
(*An over-reaction.*) Is not any artist a child of depression?
(*Then tumbling out.*) I am not rocksolid, boring, unequal to
change! I am quicksilver, I am Hermes, I laugh and I cry

and to this man I will be an equal! I will have respect!
So he hit me... I am his *maîtresse en titre.* Why should he
go to Marie-Thérèse's bed?
And he hit me... Why should he sleep with the wife of
his poet and friend?
And he hit me... Why should he open the legs of the
schoolgirls who come to gape? And he hit me... Why
should he stray his gaze in cafe, in street or in theatre,
a mutual smile, a studio visit and the evidence – a
portrait of nakedness painted in sperm.
And he slapped my face, those huge powerful hands, and
on the floor I would awake and he would watch with a
curled smile and I would scream, or whimper or make
appear that nothing had happened... and he would cuddle,
oh so lovingly he would cuddle and paint my tears and
tell me – no! – *show me* how much I was the inspiration,
how necessary I was to the ceaseless flow of his invention
and I would watch his lusting senses blaze on the fuel of
our rage as he would scream and I would scream and then
he'd take me, stoke me, stagger me and stab me gloriously
as his pencil stroked my face, my body: now dramatic,
now distorted, biting on a kerchief, head flung back, with
twisting mouth or shrieking mouth, or flaring nostrils, a
new anatomy re-arranged – should I hover like a bird... or
be gored as a minotaur, or acquire the long pointy snout
of Kasbec... his dog.

(*A beat. Honegger's Pacific 231 – Locomotive motif.*)
(*Like a snare-drum beat.*) Trouble in Spain... that big-bellied
corridor politician Franco! Federico García Lorca is
executed by firing squad but weren't we tucked away on
the Riviera!
(*Becoming expansive.*) When he was commissioned by the
Spanish Republic to make a mural for the International
Exposition in Paris, I told him: you neglect the ordinary
people, you ignore politics, you ignore suffering.
(*A beat.*)
And then they bombed Guernica.
And then his mother died.

He painted my breasts in the spiral shapes of spun-sugar
torrquellas. As a child of two, he had sketched... and
eaten. And so Spain... had died.
He was like his mother: a tyrant.
I frightened him, he said... And as with every exile, he
could cry at a distance. And he did.
(*End music.*)

So big were his tears that I had to find him another
studio. I knew the place. Could see it from the Rue de
Savoie. An enormous mansion in the Rue des Grands-
Augustins which Balzac had used as the setting for the
tale of the Unknown Masterpiece.
The irony was not lost on me...

(*Webern's orchestration of Bach's* <u>Ricercare from Musical Offering</u>.)
(*With pride.*) At each stage of the work, I photographed:
disembowelling men and beasts, a serene bull.
We are there, Marie-Thérèse and I. The battle for Spain
is the clash between us, in him. The woman with the
lamp?
At night, when I used to leave his former studio, he would
lean over the balcony, holding the lamp aloft to light my
path... a simple transposition... it's Marie-Thérèse... and the
weeping woman, holding a dead child in her arms?
(*With supreme bitterness.*) How exquisitely appropriate –
Pablo – is me.
At the time I thought it was a nice touch!...

(*With sudden bitterness.*) Who is this man, this minotaur:
Poseidon's trainee earthshaker?
(*Dryly.*) His sign is Scorpio!
He bought me a house in the county, at Ménerbes.
Infested with scorpions. Don't they love to hide in the
toilet he'd say: a sting on the balls and you're a eunuch
for life!
He had a vulgar vivacity, had this man.

(*Berg's <u>Violin Concerto</u> (1935) 'dedicated to the memory of an angel'.*)

I still live, alone, at the Rue de Savoie... and at Ménerbes. Nothing has changed.

I paint still-lives: life has stilled. Once, I was painting an alarmed clock. You paint like Cézanne, he told me. (*Sullenly.*) He only encouraged the mediocre...

(*A beat.*)

When I was a child, my bedroom door was made of glass. They could see in: and I could see out. So now my privacy I barricade. On the walls are visions and versions of myself: his lies.

(*End music.*)

(*Attempting breeziness.*) He wrote me in a play once: Desire Caught by the Tail. Another lie.

I was the edible Tart.

After the performance we went to his studio to celebrate. There were drawings for the *cognoscenti* to praise... (*An edge of pain.*)... and another face was taking my place.

In one, I was asleep and she was watching... and smiling. Dear Françoise...

He would take you to my house in Ménerbes. Within weeks you were pregnant with Claude.

(*A beat. She is almost crying but determined not to do so.*)

I lost my bicycle, but it was there all the time. I lost my dog, but when the *gendarme* brought me home, it was asleep behind the door. And I found myself, naked, sitting on the outside stairs, watching a wedding party who stared and stared – at me!

(*Convincing herself.*) My name is Theodora: a gift from God!

(*The crackle and buzz of the electroshock treatment. Messiaen's <u>Turangalila Symphony</u> creeps in. Night-time. Antibes.*)

We were walking along the beach as the fishermen shone their acetylene lamps on the water. They had tridents to spear the fascinated fish.

He painted it. Of course! Why use a net or a line when you can give the stigmata? (*An attempt at an ecclesiastical joke.*)

A tridentine mass?

(*Another buzz and crackle of electricity. She moans: it might be pain, it might be ecstasy...*)

It was the will of God. Of course I had faith. Didn't Jacques Lacan tell me so?

(*A beat.*)

Paul came to me: Nush had died. He asked me to marry him. I told him: after Picasso? Only God! Only God! Only...

(*A long despairing wail.*) God...

A diminuendo of dry, snake-rattle percussion. Then return to lilting, surging Latin-American rhythms as the lights slowly fade to blackness.

The End.

FRANÇOISE

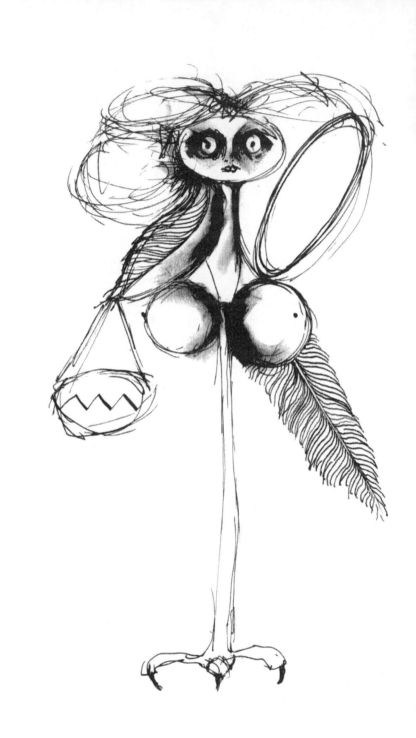

Even today, critics and scholars routinely describe Françoise Gilot's book 'Life with Picasso' as a settling of old scores. She has been reviled for writing a bitchy, malicious volume in which, apart from everything else, Picasso is made to speak in a manner which, it is claimed, was singularly inaccurate. This is ironic. Douglas Cooper, for example, savages Gilot but praises Geneviève Laporte's memoir which makes Picasso speak in the same manner as Gilot – except that Gilot makes Picasso speak intelligently in paragraphs whereas Laporte retails tittle-tattle in short sentences.

To someone living in a normal world, this is strange: strange because Gilot wrote a book on Picasso that is not only – and in my view unquestionably – the best book written on him by any of his 'women' or his associates (male or female), but is also one of the three or four really illuminating books written on him by anyone.

Gilot had numerous advantages. She was a) highly intelligent b) a painter herself and c) well-read, d) she was closely associated with Picasso for roughly ten years and unlike Dora or Marie-Thérèse, had actually lived with Pablo on a day-to-day basis. None of these points stood in the way of bitter 'critical' denunciations.

Many of the people who vilified Gilot knew perfectly well that she was telling the truth. The historian James Lord even said so in one of the few positive reviews of the book. On a broader front the art-trade was well aware that Picasso himself was rather less than a saint. The magisterial Picasso scholar from New York's MOMA, Alfred H. Barr, Jr., is quoted in the archives as stating that 'Picasso is not a reasonable man and the immense diet of flattery he has fed on, his age and his sense of power, have increased since 1939.' He wrote that in 1954.

Not that you would be aware of this from the hagiographical gush that has masqueraded, over the years, as Picasso biography and memoir. Anyone who has read the literature should be perfectly aware that, as Françoise has said, Pablo simply made up stories for writers and critics, either amusing himself at their expense, or telling them what they wanted to hear. Fiction is often more useful to commerce than fact.

Likewise, anyone should have been able to figure out that Picasso's comments on Françoise (Sample: Poor Françoise, she makes a drama out of everything) were simply a projection of his own failings onto the woman who had the good sense to leave him. It is surely no accident that he suffered one creative crisis after another while he was with her. One might say that – for once – he had come up against a woman who would not be consumed by his fire.

Although Françoise is still alive, a point which I have tried to ignore but which has probably influenced, at a subconscious level, the choices that I have made as a dramatist, I have tried to deal with her in exactly the same manner as I have dealt with all of the others: to view her sympathetically; to see things from her point of view; to uncover her perspectives upon herself and upon Pablo. But this is my construction of Françoise. In the monologue she is, as with the others, dead.

Staging: I have opted for a very precise use of full-size cut-outs, which can be flown from the Gods or otherwise moved onto the stage. I'd suggest that the designer look at the appropriate Picasso images and then make his or her own versions.

~

Darkness.

We hear the theme from the Jean Cocteau film, <u>Beauty and the Beast</u>, composed by Georges Auric.

As light, very slowly, begins to rinse the stage, we discover FRANÇOISE, energetically working a footpump. She is blowing up a life-size female nude.

This is a task which she addresses in a business-like fashion. She occasionally stops to inspect a flabby breast or a sagging buttock.

When the nude is fully inflated she stands back to admire her work, then discovers the audience. She looks from one to the other.

FRANÇOISE: (*Peremptorily.*) *Don't* ask! (*A beat.*) Later...
(*Clicks her fingers: music stops abruptly in mid bar.*) You know what you've been listening to?
(*Shakes her head in disbelief. Then engagingly.*) Cretins!
It's *Beauty and the Beast.* The music for Cocteau's movie.
Guess which part Pablo played?

(*Picks on one of the males in the audience.*) I see you're displaying an unusual interest in artificial sex-aids.
Thought you'd wandered into a brothel, did you?
Couldn't believe your luck?

I suppose the only difference between you and Pablo was that Pablo could afford to do what he liked, in all senses of the words... well, kinda the only difference.
He was after all *the* major artist of the twentieth century. And didn't he know it!
He was also a major, majorly definitive... bastard.
God, I must get rid of these Americanisms!
God is very definitely not an American.
Unfortunately he's not French either.

(*Ruminatively.*) Being dead... is a problem for me, if not for you. If I were a French *philosophe*, or semiotician, a structuralist or a sociologist, I could swathe my thoughts in a thickly spun web of impenetrability. Therefore no need to interrogate them closely; and no need to worry about communication. Like Alice, words would mean whatever the reader or listener wanted them to mean; or thought they meant.
Fortunately – for you – I am not a French *philosophe.*

(*Amused.*) I know. You are saying to yourselves: who is this woman? What is the size of the chip she has upon her shoulder?
Your language is so strange: if you eat chips, why have them upon the shoulder? (*Shrugs.*) Trying to understand the English is an impossibility.
At least in America people are direct, forceful, willing to praise.
I enjoyed living there.
And American English is so much more... sensible... than the British variety.
Much less complication. And they know how to spell!

Chips.
The myth of Ariadne.

I once wrote an autobiographical book about my life with Picasso.

137

The scholars went to town.
Mister Penrose decreed that it was 'in bad taste'.
Mister Cooper decided that it was 'spiteful but discredited'.
Mister Cooper's long-time house-companion, John
Richardson, complained that it was 'the more
unconscionable as Picasso loathes any public divulgence
of his private views.'
Oh, and the ever-so-holy Pierre Daix called me 'an
embittered busybody', displaying spitefulness and venom.
Little shits. Even my one-time *amie*, the painter André
Marchand, chastised me: I should not 'confuse petty
personal affairs with the grand adventure of a creator'.

Petty? Ha!
Wasn't I properly ticked off for daring to make a public
exposure of a private life!
A private life carefully cocooned for the consumption of
the masses.
A private life presented for the adoring gaze.
A private life in which The Master was assumed upwards
and outwards, arms raised to give benediction.
Pablo as God: Father, Son and Holy Ghost; Christ and
the Anti-Christ; Buddha and Brahma.
Pablo as the riddle of the sphinx.

(*A beat.*) There's a beautiful Egyptian sculpture, called
The Seated Scribe. It's only twenty inches high. Painted
limestone.
I used to visit it all the time. In the Louvre.
When I first met Pablo, it was as if the statue had come
to life. The same broad shoulders; the same staring,
basilisk eyes; the same geometry of the head, squashing
down the neck; the same ironic smile playing about the
corners of the lips.

Art and the art of biography and autobiography.
Wasn't I just a woman – someone who had slept with
Picasso, a mistress, and therefore a tart, and therefore
a liar?

(*With brio.*) Was it relevant that I had been the companion of this man for almost ten years?

Of course not!

That I had lived with him for almost seven years.

That I had borne him children?

That I was a painter myself and therefore well-placed to comment upon his art?

Stuff and nonsense.

That I had sat in studios posing, watching him paint, giving him suggestions and ideas, even painting replicas of a day's work so that he could take it in a different direction; and therefore was better placed than almost anyone else to understand the way he worked?

Of no value.

That I tried to understand his character, explore his motivations, reveal his behaviour?

Pah!

What business had I to write about the Great Man when such as Penrose, Daix, Cooper and Richardson should, could, would – and did – do it for me?

One man supported me. A biographer called James Lord. He replied wasn't it significant that Richardson in his review, never categorically stated that the portrait of Picasso was a false one!

Mister Lord said, and so I quote, that 'he neglects to do so, I believe, for the excellent reason that he is in a position to know how astonishingly true to life the portrait is.'

(*Gently.*) And it was.

Within limits.

I wasn't actually trying to harm Pablo.

Which was why I suppressed anything that I could not document at the time.

I was trying to understand him; to separate him from the carapace of fawning, adulatory, and dishonest flattery that thickened with every month that passed.

In return he instigated three legal actions in an attempt to ban the book.

139

Ask yourself why.
Of course he lost all of them.

(*To the sound of Poulenc's <u>Mouvements Perpetuels</u> a life-size cut-out of a voluptuous nude, descends from the Gods: the legs are splayed open, and marked attention has been paid to the genitalia in a scribble of black charcoal. The face is blank.*)
Make no mistake. Pablo was a genius.
Cruel, sentimental, ruthless, perverse and promiscuous.
But as an artist – he was a genius who wrote his autobiography in his work.
For a long time I saw the artist, but I didn't see the man.
And yes, I had known of Dora, Marie-Thérèse, Olga, Fernande...
But I was twenty, a tom-boy. I thought I could take on the world and win!
I wanted to believe in Pablo.
I wanted to bask in the charm, to breathe in the aphrodisiac of power.
I wanted to get off on the excitement of the unpredictable.

(*She takes out a bright red lipstick, goes over to the blow-up doll and rouges the nipples.*)
For Pablo, painting and making love were the same thing.
How was I to know that Pablo's imagination, and therefore his painting, and so Pablo himself, would turn into this?
(*She has rouged the two 'lips' of a vaginal mouth onto the doll.*)

Pablo always loved the human body... (*Amused.*) was always... fascinated by the sexual organs... and I... for a while... loved Pablo.
I didn't... at the start.
At the start it was a game...

(*Some bright and brittle Poulenc.*)
(*She goes over to a cafe table, sits down and sips her glass of wine.*)
(*Conversationally.*) My friend Geneviève was sitting here (*Points to other side of table.*) with the actor Alain Cuny

in the middle. We were having dinner.

It was during the German occupation of France and we were in a black market restaurant called Le Catalan – the only bistro in the area where you could get a juicy steak without coupons.

I knew Picasso would be there. His studio was in the same street: Rue des Grands-Augustins.

Over there (*Points to other side of stage.*) Monsieur Picasso was entertaining his friends.

I knew he was watching us. His voice just that little bit louder than necessary so that we could hear each of his *bon mots*. The Spanish accent as thick as a paella.

The famous black lock that I had seen in so many photographs had vanished.

Instead of a thick glossy luxuriance, his hair was thinning and brushed with grey. Underneath, the face became vacant, mask like: at intervals... just like my statue of the Seated Scribe.

I wondered if he were being bored.

(*Enjoying herself.*) Dora Maar, his current mistress, was at the table.

She was as immobile as my Egyptian statue. I recognized her from the paintings. Gossip had it that she was on the way out.

Then there was Marie-Laure, the Vicomtesse de Noailles, whose elongated face was framed by an ornate coiffure as if she were some decadent eighteenth-century courtesan in search of stimulation.

(*Rising.*) And yes, I should have seen him for what he was, his iconography etched in the image before me. But we all see different images, don't we?

What did I see?

I saw the painter that André Marchand, my painter *ami* saw.

I saw the painter that my young teacher Endre Rozsda saw.

I saw the most influential painter that century – the man

who could give me the key to the doors of perception. I saw the myth of Ariadne!

I saw a man old enough to be my father but who radiated energy, power, passion, sex; a man whom everyone in the restaurant wanted to meet; a man who had authority, stature, fame; a man whose hands could mould any shape, draw any form, imagine what had not yet been imagined. I saw a man to whom money, the war, and the world were nothing.

(*Acting it out.*) He stood up suddenly and without so much as a look at his companions he carried a bowl of cherries over to our table, nodded at Alain whom he knew, and offered us some. Alain introduced us. I told the cherry-carrier that we were painters whereupon he burst out laughing.

'Girls who look like that can't be painters' – (*an aside to audience.*) looking at Alain.

'Perhaps that's why we're having a joint exhibition at the Decré's Gallery in Rue Boissy d'Anglas,' I responded tartly.

He stared down at me: black sloe eyes, drinking me in.

'Well, I'm a painter too. Isn't that a coincidence! You can come to my studio and see some of *my* paintings!'

Naturally I paused and looked uninterested for a moment.

'When?' Very casual.

'Tomorrow. Whenever you want...'

Smiling, he turned and carried his bowl of cherries back to his friends.

Waste not, want not.

It's so satisfying to hook a fish, isn't it?

Yes. We were both fishing. Playing a game.

(*A touch of Chabrier.*)

My father was a difficult man. Solitary. Used to take me hunting, sailing... wanted me to be a boy, to face up

to any kind of fear. So I became fascinated with whatever
I feared. He decided that I would be a lawyer, sent me to
the Sorbonne.
I had never lacked for money. He indulged me in what
he deemed to be my hobby, even paid for my Hungarian
art teacher. But when war came and my friends went into
the Resistance one by one, and when Geneviève became
a pupil of the artist Maillol, I decided to pursue my
vocation: Art!

Mon père... was not amused. First of all he sent my
mother to convince me otherwise. Then he threatened to
have me committed.
I ran around to my grandmother's and darted upstairs.
He followed me: powerful, persistent, implacable, his
frame filling the space on the stairway... as stocky as
Pablo's...
I tried to dodge past but his fists were faster, hitting me
on shoulders, face and back as I slid to the ground,
shoving my legs and arms through the banisters so that
he could no longer hit my face.
Out of the corner of my eye I could see little rivulets of
blood, sloping down the white of the banisters, hear the
tiny plop as the drops rippled out across my knee.
My grandmother arrived... My allowance stopped.

Playing a game.
Mon père considered that he had rights. Over me.
Perhaps he thought that with so much expenditure of effort,
of money, of time – didn't he organise my education, hire
tutors, toughen me up in the world of the great outdoors –
that I was his possession?
In business, papa isolated a need, then fulfilled it. He
always used the best talent; bought the best whether it
was furniture or a suit.
I had a need: art. I determined the best: Picasso.
Therefore, Picasso was going to be my teacher.

My friend Geneviève was prettier than me. But I was more intelligent than her.

And I *was* pretty.

So we went to 7 Rue des Grands-Augustins, Geneviève and me, into the lair with the secretary, Sabartés, as a half-blind Cerberus at the door of the anteroom.

Light flooded in from a tall window, illuminating the dull red octagonal tiles, the turtle doves, the spiky green plants. Sabartés, like a prelate shuffling down cathedral aisles, led us into a long room with a long table like an altar, piled high with books, photos, hats, magazines, a piece of crystal the size of a pumpkin.

I nearly tripped over an object at the door to the next room. It was dull and brown and bronze: a skull, announcing itself as the life and death of its creator whose sculptural works were splayed out in the next room: a Marie-Thérèse head, *Man with a Sheep*, not to mention a raft of junk including handlebars and rolls of canvas.

On the walls, his collector's instinct played with colour as against the austerity of the sculpture: Modigliani, Vuillard, Douanier Rousseau, and a Matisse *Still-Life*, staining the shadows with pink, orange and ultramarine.

Ten minutes later, when Picasso was showing us around, he ensconced himself on a Louis XIII table. He was wearing a sailor's jersey, in blue stripes, and a very old pair of baggy trousers. 'This', he said casually, 'was where I painted *Guernica*.'

We were impressed.

Guernica.

Imagine... (*a long beat.*)

I tried to imagine my father, dressed in old trousers and a sailor's jersey, casually sitting on a Louis XIII table... I tried to imagine him as a world-famous artist. I tried.

Picasso was sixty-three. Older than my father. I was twenty-one.

And I was enjoying myself!

I started to go to the Picasso residence on my own.
In the mornings he saw people: fuel for his work. In the
afternoons he *made* his work. Soon I was coming to him
in the afternoons, carrying my canvases under my arm,
listening to him as he recreated, only for me, the origins
of his most famous paintings.
Of course I knew he was interested in more than my art.
We were playing a game as elaborate and formal as a
Renaissance dance: advance, withdraw; display ardour, then
indifference; excite him, detumesce him!

Once I arrived, having bicycled over, my hair soaking
from an afternoon shower.
He took me to the bathroom and gently dried my hair.
Another time, on the pretence of showing me the view
from the roof, he came up behind me on the stairs and
cupped his hands around my breasts.
I acted as if nothing had happened.
Then he showed me his 'museum': a wooden Egyptian
foot; various cigar boxes which he opened, to reveal tiny
stage sets complete with painted cut-out actors...
We were the actors and the room was the stage set.

Suddenly turning, he kissed me full on the mouth.
I simply accepted it.
'You're supposed to make seduction *difficult* for me!'
I smiled politely at him.
'You may do with me as you will.'
That flummoxed him.

Once he bade me strip. So I did. He sat me on his knee.
He knew that I would go to bed with him if he wished it.
But he wanted more. Intelligent, and clever.
He lay me on his bed and gently caressed me as if he
were creating a living sculpture.
I couldn't believe how gentle he was. My nipples were
as erect as tent-pegs and when he stroked my pubic hair

I could feel my mound swelling and wanting, waiting to be fulfilled.
He told me to put my clothes back on.
Clever, clever man.

But I intended to win. On my terms.
He took me round the journey of his past:
Montparnasse... the studios of Utrillo and Modigliani... Montmartre and the Bateau Lavoir.
It was the golden age for him. For me it was damp dirty walls, wide rickety floorboards, and the stale foetid smell of decay.
He knocked at the door of his old studio, then tried to open it, but the door to the Blue Period remained locked away, hidden on the other side of peeling paint... and damp door jambs...

At intervals I would simply... vanish.
Absence is a useful tool for a young girl. And with Pablo, one needed to keep one's wits about one. One needed an edge.
Of course it was only a matter of time before I was sleeping with him.
This seemed perfectly reasonable.
After all, he could sleep with whomever he wanted to. And he wanted me! Regularly.

He too played the game.
'Don't think you mean anything to me!'
'Really?'
'I like my independence.'
'So do I!' I told him tartly, and vanished for three months!

(*As if surprised with herself.*) But I kept coming back.
He wanted me to move in with him but I kept on refusing. You know what it's like when you gorge on chocolate, even though you know you shouldn't? An illicit thrill... and Pablo was dangerous, illicit, powerful...

and very good in bed, or out of it... gentle and tender...
hard and driving, orgasm and... orgasm...

But I kept him dangling.
He started turning up in my studio, surprising me in an
old peignoir and rumpled hair.
It was March, 1946 when he went for checkmate: seduction
by art.
My *annus mirabilis.*

He arrived with a child's sketchpad which had a drawing
of a rooster on the cover. Typical Pablo! Wasn't the first
painting of his that he showed me, on my first ever visit
to his studio, that of a cock crowing lustily!
The cock had come in search of the hen!

'You sketch: I sketch – a dialogue!'
And we did. He did portraits of me. *I* did portraits of me.
It was the first of a series of sketchbooks.
A collaboration!

*She approaches the voluptuous nude and proceeds to sketch in two
circumflex accents as eyebrows on the empty face. The nose is
two parallel lines. The mouth a ripe three lines.   Based on the signs
that Picasso evolved as a notation for FRANÇOISE's face: see
for example the sketchbook face reproduced in 'The Sketchbooks
of Picasso', p.270.*

He was exploring my face, evolving a notation. So my
eyebrows became circumflex accents... I watched him
explore my surface, approach each nook and cranny,
try different characterisations as when, at his request,
I braided my hair, Russian spy fashion...

It was a while before he realised that I had been doing the
same, with *him*, from memory, for the past three years.
The man as different varieties of the mask.
Never give away too much – at the start.

(*We hear Cyril Scott's Bells from 'Five Poems' [Valentines album.*
Troy 071] which runs underneath.)
Pablo was being very, very persistent.
I should move in with him. It was my duty.
He needed me. He might not have that many years left.
I needed a break from Pablo.

Unexpectedly it arrived in the form of a broken arm when
I fell down the stairs in my grandmother's. Electricity
shortages in the post-war years!
Grandmaman took me to Antibes but not before Pablo
arrived with a huge Azalea, blooming with bright red
flowers, and pink and blue ribbons. Absurdly hideous!
Clever, clever man.
One forgets flowers, but not this monstrous display of
deliberate bad taste!

Not far from Antibes was Monsieur Fort, the retired
engraver who had printed so many of Vollard's editions,
including Pablo's *Les Saltimbanques.* He still had his
hand-presses and copper plates.
(*Fade music.*)
'If you're going to the Midi, might as well learn something
while you're there.'
Pablo of course, teaching me the one great lesson: if
you're an artist, there's no such thing as rest and play.
He rented the upper floors of the house for me and soon
grandmaman was left in Antibes while I discovered the
world of etching needles, burnishers, scrapers, copper-
plates, and how to bite into them with acid... all under
the tutelage of an eighty-year old man, bent over like an
olive tree in the wake of the *mistral.*
I began to realise why Pablo always liked artisans: a
lifetime of experience to be tapped into and used.

I wrote to Pablo telling him that there was no point in
coming down to see me.
Monsieur Fort was a fine teacher and I was working well.

Besides, my friend Geneviève had come to visit me.
He arrived two days later.

Geneviève was not amused.
She told me what happened when I went off to visit my
grandmother.
Pablo, proffering a copperplate, matter-of-factly says, 'I'll
give you an etching lesson', sits her down at the edge of
the bed and follows it up with 'I'll give you a baby now.
That's what you need!'
Pablo of course just wanted to get rid of her.
He only wanted me.

Geneviève tells me that I must come home with her.
Tomorrow.
I go to see Pablo.
'How can you believe a girl who tries to seduce me
behind your back?'
'Geneviève doesn't lie! I'm going with her.'
'There's got to be an unnatural relationship between you
two. No other explanation'.
I giggled. 'You should have been a Jesuit!'
At one point he unbuckled his belt and raged: 'Is this all a
game for you? Don't I mean anything to you? You have to
come and live with me!'
Pathetic.
But I didn't think so at the time.
I thought he must have been very much in love with me,
to let himself be seen in such an unfavourable light.
An hour later he was at the 'I don't have many more years
to live' stage.
Obviously wanting me. Badly. Contrite. Soft.
And he *had* come all the way to the Midi.
I decided to stay with him.
'You're sleepwalking,' pronounced Geneviève. And left.

(*Another touch of Chabrier.*)
Pablo took me to visit Matisse who was living in a house

in Venice, near the Dominican chapel which he would
decorate two years later.

Imagine. Meeting Matisse. Me.

Monsieur Matisse was in bed, using scissors to make
paper cut-outs.

At one point he remarked that if he made a portrait of
me, he would make my hair green.

'Why would you want to make a portrait of *her*?'

'She's a head that interests me. Those circumflex eyebrows!'

Pablo was not amused. Grumbled about it for ages.

'I don't make portraits of *his* woman, do I?'

We went back to Paris but the exchange had rankled.

Now he, Pablo, was going to make my portrait and it
would outdo Matisse!

Annus mirabilis!

I moved in with him. For a month we scarcely ever left
the house.

'I rarely work from the model, but as you're here...'

I posed nude. For one hour. He observed. Not so much as
a pencil in his hand.

'You can dress now. I see what I have to do. You won't
have to pose again.'

(*To Debussy's <u>Petite Suite for Piano Duet</u> – First Movement: En
Bateau – a life-size cutout of Picasso's Femme-Fleur [or a version
of same] slowly descends from the Gods, centre-rear.*)

The next day he produced a series of drawings. Of me.
From memory.

Then a series of eleven lithographs of my head.

Then, still on the same day, he started work on *La Femme
Fleur*.

It didn't always look like that.

I asked him if I could watch.

Four weeks! Two in the afternoon until eleven at night,
usually without a break! It started as a more-or-less
realistic portrait of myself, seated in a chair.

Not for long!

'Somehow, I don't see you seated. Too independent!'
I rose from the ashes of the seat; blossomed into
the vertical.
Then it came to him.
'Matisse isn't the only one who could paint you with
green hair!'

For Pablo's mind had sparked into the metaphor of hair as
leaves, which led him, inevitably, into woman as flower.
He painted over the chair, my legs, and my bust, with a
light background colour.
There was no palette. Just a small table covered with
newspapers.
A thin rooted stalk developed, topped like a sunflower
with head and leaves.
In his search for the head, he cut out various shapes in
sky-blue paper, sketched in signs for mouth, nose and
eyes, then pinned them to the canvas until he found the
right form. What Matisse could do!...

He would stand in front of the canvas for three, even
four hours.
No movement was superfluous.
Around the base of the easel were cans holding gray or
neutral colours.
Pure colour he squeezed from the tube.
'There must be darkness everywhere, except on the
canvas. You have to be hypnotised by your work'.
He was. And I was.
Watching myself emerge, cut-down, taken apart,
re-painted, reformed, transformed and translated, slowly
stripped back to an essence: the straight line of nose, the
curve of eyebrow, the pout of a mouth and the wide
openness of an eye. Femininity in pastel colour; youth
and fecundity blossoming into flower.

But I was still... uncertain.

I wouldn't give myself to him upon demand, which used to infuriate him: weren't there dozens of women, daily, only too ready to drop their knickers upon the flicker of an eyelid?

(*A touch of Ravel's* <u>*Le Tombeau de Couperin*</u>.)
Yet this was the man whom The Museum of Modern Art in New York had just honoured by publishing the book *Picasso: Fifty Years of His Art.*
A dozen copies had arrived for him.
The appendices alone listed his theatre productions, illustrations, exhibitions, works by him in American collections, even a chronology of the places where he had lived.
I read the opening paragraph: 'Probably no painter in history has been so much written about – attacked and defended, explained and obscured, slandered and honoured...' The bibliography listed over five hundred and fifty major items, including forty-six monographs! And the subject of all of this acclaim was living with me, drawing me, painting me into history, teaching me, needing me, loving me...

But, wasn't Dora still around – she who dismissed me as 'that schoolgirl' and who sweetly said to Pablo, head glancing in my direction, 'in bed, but not at the table'. Pablo always liked to take his revenge.
We're going to the Midi for the summer he stated, slyly informing me that we were going first to Dora Maar's house in Ménerbes.
'I bought it for her, so why shouldn't I use it?'
How to torture Dora.

It was a warning sign – we never notice warning signs, do we?
But they come back to haunt us.
When Pablo was doing lithographs of me at the dark, dank and ramshackle world of Monsieur Mourlot's,

I would talk to the artisans. Many of the lithographic
stones had been in use since the early nineteenth century.
Since they were made of limestone and so porous, the
ink from an impression would penetrate beneath the
surface. Often, scores of years later, a portion of a
drawing would resurface, the stone's memory, a slippage
between past and present.
I had lots of slippages, but instead of lodging in the
forefront of the transferred drawing, they sank into
the porous depths, waiting for experience to say 'I told
you so'...

(*A low percussive underbeat.*)
Ménerbes.
Strangely, or so it seemed at the time, Marie-Thérèse
seemed to know where he was. Daily letters were arriving.
Pablo would go on long walks, reading these missives,
then upon his return would quote whole paragraphs of
adulatory and amorous prose.
'You wouldn't write to me like that!'
'True!'
'You don't love me enough!'
Ménerbes: hot, dusty, boring, and full of scorpions, even
in the bedroom.
I was leaning against a rock once when he yelled out.
I turned to see three scorpions basking above my head.
'My sign of the zodiac,' he said complacently.

At night we would be walking along the deserted, winding
roads, the darkness as thick as one of Dora Maar's fur coats.
Might catch a glimpse of a scrawny cat, skulking in the
roadway until without warning, in a flurry of swooshing
wings, the tawny whirr of an owl would pounce, claws
picking up the cat, cat's claws scratching for a foothold on
the white ruff, and battle would commence!
Pablo was entranced. Cat and owl. Bull and bull-fighter.
Death in the raw.

(*A touch of Poulenc's Toccata from* <u>*Trois Pièces*</u>.)
I'd had enough of this hostile environment: I'd
hitch-hike to Marseilles and – but hardly had I sat at the
edge of the road before who should drive up but Pablo...
He was very sweet. Was I being bored? I needed a child!
We started to laugh.
An old friend of his, Marie Cuttoli arrived and invited
us to visit her at Cap d'Antibes. Why ever not!
Yes! Fine linen. A comfortable bed. Waiter service!
And yes, we could stay on, go to Monsieur Fort's, sunbathe
at the beach... so we did. And women, young women,
attractive women, would come up to him, lying there
half-naked on the sand, and coyly ask for his autograph.
Even in front of me!
And he would oblige, often leaning forward, cupping a
hand around a firm leg or a slender waist, and he would
write his autograph on bare suntanned flesh and at the
end of the morning we would slide into bed and I was
pregnant in no time at all.
(*A beat: end of percussive undertow*.)

I know. But I allowed it to happen. Twice in fact.
One always repeats the same mistakes.
Sunshine and sex. Sunshine and thunder.

It was odd. We lived at Monsieur Fort's.
Now there was a man with an idiosyncratic eye for
decoration.
The bedroom was painted in royal blue, the ceiling ablaze
with white stars edged in red, and the bed faced a huge
bay window overlooking the rolling, whispering sea.
At night you could hear the tinkle of the boats, moored
along the shore.
The furniture was painted red with a ceiling rhyme of
white stars.
I thought it was bad taste at the time: Pablo's azalea
without the irony.
What I didn't see was the red face, white hair and

blue eyes of Monsieur Fort writing their signature after
a lifetime of being hemmed in as an artisan.
What I didn't see, and what I think Pablo saw, was the
world of eternity, made manifest in a bedroom, a world
held at bay by an ejaculation of starry nights.

Sunshine and sex.
Pablo's only problem was lack of space to paint.
Without the one and the other, the painting and the sex,
he became morose.
So when he was offered an atelier in the Musée
d'Antibes Pablo was itching to get started. We went
over to visit, and were shown around by the curator,
the extravagantly named Monsieur Jules-César
Romuald Dor de la Souchère.
Naturally he had been a teacher of Greek and Latin at a
nearby lycée.
And he had a passion, having spent years
reconstructing the history of the town, translating
Greek and Roman inscriptions, medieval parchments,
restoring the Grimaldi Castle which was now the
museum. He took us onto the ramparts, the terrace
which once had been the Acropolis of Antipolis,
showed us the classical casts.
My father had taught me the world of the mythological
Gods and now this man was making them manifest.
Ariadne...

In front of me Pablo, from his rutting depths, allowed this
world to surface. He wasn't going to paint a few pictures.
He was going to decorate the walls of a museum! Nymphs,
fauns, centaurs and satyrs, a Mediterranean mythology
dominated by the Flower-Woman.
Me!
And I was still learning.

Be flexible. Interrogate your ideas. Suit the practice to
the place.

Antibes was incandescent in summer, wind-iced in
winter. Lapped by a restless sea.
So Pablo, for his supports, selected wood used for fishing
boats; fibro-cement panels, used in houses, for his painting
surface; and cans of boat-paint along with ordinary
paintbrushes for his artist supplies!

The following summer, shortly after Claude was born,
we were back. Pablo painted a final panel, the Antibes
Museum now became The Picasso Museum, and Pablo
discovered ceramics at Vallauris, 'the city of gold'. At
any rate he turned a dying town into the new ceramic
goldrush and we ended up in a cold, drafty version of
ugliness called La Galloise.

Children.
Annus mirabilis replaced by *annus horribilis.*
It was the child.
Not the fault of the child, but Pablo's response to me
after the child.
Maybe having one gives such a different perspective that
the old certainties disintegrate...

Maybe Pablo couldn't cope with my attention being
focussed on Claude.
Maybe I simply became the functionary: the woman who
cooked and cleaned and lit the fires, changed nappies,
got up in the night when Pablo woke me, convinced that
Claude was choking to death.
Not that he'd ever go look himself.
What else is a woman for?
And hadn't I started to paint again, locking myself in a
room every hour I could get?
You have to be tough to live with a man like Picasso.
And I was not about to go under.

Pablo was working methodically at ceramics, changing
the language of clay and glaze.
Minor work. He knew it himself. 'An object but not

necessarily an objet d'art.'
But he was obsessive about everything. I had asked him
for a house and got it: La Galloise. I was pregnant again
within a month.

He took himself off to Poland with Marcel, his chauffeur.
The Congress of Intellectuals for Peace. Four days he
said. He was gone three weeks.
Pablo never could believe that a woman could be
anything but overjoyed by his mere presence. Oh I got
daily telegrams. My name misspelt. With the salutation
'*Bons Baisers*' as if I were a tart. Marcel had obviously
been delegated.

On the day Pablo came back, he walked up the flight of
steps to the house, beaming. He opened his arms as if
to give me a hug so I slapped him across the side of his
face. There was a satisfying smack.
'Do that again and I'll leave!'
Turning on my heel I went and locked myself in
my room.
He was nice as ninepence in the morning!

We were cordial from then on. I didn't realise that he had
begun to see other women.
About two weeks before the birth, the doctor told me to
leave for the clinic at once.
I asked for the car. 'Call an ambulance,' he replied.
Marcel told him that he could drop me off en route.
'Drop me off first. I don't want to be late. Then you can
come back for her'.

Paloma was born. He began to go off for days on end.
Still I didn't suspect.
When Paul Éluard remarried in 1951, in Saint Tropez,
we went to his wedding.
A week later he was down there again, living with
the Cantal cheese: Geneviève Laporte.
It was the woman who owned the ceramics factory at

Vallauris who told me: I'd never liked her.
I simply worked. Pablo denied everything.
And I had my reward when Kahnweiler took me on as
one of his stable (and hadn't he refused Dora Maar!) and
gave me an exhibition in 1952. I was financially secure
at long last.

(*A snatch of Stravinsky's percussive* __Les Noces__ *as a full-size cutout of
a Picasso 'Artist' descends from the Gods, close to FRANÇOISE.
The testicles are prominent.*)
Pablo's affairs began to be reported in the papers. He even
signed into hotels with his own name. But still he denied it.
I began to address him as 'Vous', instead of 'Tu'.
That annoyed him.
And I continued to work. My children rarely saw him
unless he wanted a model, or needed a photograph of the
Loving Father to bolster up the Picasso Legend.
More and more I began to think: Lithographs. The
stone's memory. Slippage.

Elements, to which I had paid no attention at the time,
seeped upwards and outwards.
Pablo's cache of manuscripts by Apollinaire. When the
Pléiade edition of his works was in train, the editor came
to Pablo to gain access to this unpublished work.
Pablo refused: too much trouble.
Pierre Colle, Max Jacob's literary executor, coming to
Rue des Grands-Augustins and asking Pablo to use
his quite considerable authority with the Germans to
intercede for Max who was in a concentration camp.
No need, said Pablo. Max can fly.
His soul did. From the camp.

Pablo's old trunk, stuffed with five or six million francs,
and Pablo counting them, again and again, like a child
hoarding marbles.
Chagall's daughter, telling Pablo that her father's wife
had left him and Pablo laughing. 'It could happen

to you,' she said. 'Not a chance,' replied Pablo.
Me telling Pablo I would leave him. 'Don't imagine
people will be interested in you. You're only of interest
inasmuch as you have had access to me!'
'God is really only another artist. He creates camels,
dogs, zebras. No taste you see!'

When my mother died, my father, to whom I hadn't
spoken in over ten years, invited me back to his home.
He always was direct, my father.
'Picasso. He's an intelligent man. He could have been
discreet, but he wasn't.
So he wanted you to find out.
If you want to leave him, I'll make sure that the children
are secure financially.'
Strange, isn't it.
This man, my father, in so many ways a Pablo but
without the gift, grew into some kind of humanity
whereas the artist did the reverse...

September the third, 1953.
'I took the children and left him. He shouted 'Fuck you!'
from the steps.
And yet... it was almost as if he admired me for leaving.
Not that he made it easy.
I married a childhood friend, a promising painter. One
by one, all avenues closed.
Pablo had put out the word.
Kahnweiler got rid of me. No galleries would show
either myself or my husband Luc.
I watched as his career ground slowly towards zero.
It made things difficult between us.
Luc, who had been a father towards Pablo's children, was
being ground down... by Pablo.
When Pablo paints, he paints with other people's blood.

(*A touch of Debussy's La Mer.*)
When I was a girl, I had always loved the myth of
Ariadne.

You remember her? She was the one who guided Theseus
out of the labyrinth after he had slain the Minotaur.
When I met Pablo, perhaps I thought that I could help
him slay the Minotaur in himself and guide him out of
his labyrinth.
Ironically, of course, she saved his life, only to be
abandoned on the island of Naxos.

When I was living with my grandmother, I painted a
mural in my room.
It was of Ariadne, deserted by her lover. Descending
from Mount Olympus is the God Dionysus, determined
to save her, and make her his wife.
Wasn't it obvious, I thought.
Dionysus, the infernal deity, all instinct and insatiable
libido, captures rational, ordered Ariadne in the shape
of me.
Of course I still had gotten it wrong.
Pablo was Dionysus; and Theseus; and the Minotaur!

He had refused to acknowledge the children.

One day he phoned me. Out of the blue. If I really
wanted, he would marry me.
For the sake of the children. Legitimacy for the
children.
It took my breath away.

(*She walks over to the cut-out of the artist, picking up a large pair
of scissors from the table as she passes.*)
(*Thoughtfully, she carefully snips off its testicles, one by one.*)
Legitimacy.
My children finally recognised by their father.
And if I married Pablo, all the impediments to Luc's
career, all of the hurts that he had so unflinchingly
withstood, would vanish.
The painter would arise like the phoenix.

I started divorce proceedings, and so informed Pablo's lawyers.
Within a few months the children would be re-united with their father, my career could start to blossom once again, and life with Pablo... well, it wouldn't be so bad. He had asked *me*... back...

Less than one month later, in secret, and without so much as a by-your-leave to his lawyers, Pablo married Jacqueline. (*A very long beat.*)

I should have known better. Shouldn't I?
(*She takes a bite out of one of the 'testicles', then spits it out.*)
Great art!
Pity about the man.

Ariadne?
Tough shit!

Turning on her heel, she strides over to the blow-up nude and pulls the cap off the air-nozzle. The lights begin to dim. She watches a second as it deflates, then almost jauntily walks towards an exit. Almost as an afterthought, she turns.

And no – he didn't have the last laugh. It took a long while but finally I became whole again, and remarried, and stayed married, until the day that I died.

As the lights fade to blackness we hear the theme music to Cocteau's <u>Beauty and the Beast</u> rise and swell into the darkness.

The End.

JACQUELINE

It is always dangerous to take art critics, curators, indeed anyone in the art world, too seriously. The major problem in relation to Picasso is that everyone had something to gain from him, and therefore most of them had a vested interest in manipulating the truth. Jacqueline earned fulsome, indeed cloying tributes from a welter of eminent curators, critics, and other assorted specimens from the arts, including John Richardson. This didn't stop Mr Richardson from describing her – once Jacqueline was safely dead – as 'the unhappy widow who was to emerge in all her malevolence after the artist's death.' But then again, there are fortunes to be made and careers to be brokered. It is, however, worth asking a simple question: would Picasso or Jacqueline for that matter, have become the people they became if they had not been force-fed on an endless diet of unalloyed, dishonest, none-too-disinterested flattery – often by the very people whom one would expect to possess some integrity of opinion and judgement, both moral and artistic?

From the outside Jacqueline can seem a very unattractive character. She certainly was single-minded. She certainly set her cap at Picasso. But then again she was encouraged to do so by a wide range of people who did not seem to be above pandering – in every sense – to an old man, to ensure his continued production and their continued profit.

Indisputably she was a good wife to Picasso in the practical sense – she took exemplary care of him. In my opinion, while not being intellectually orientated, she was nevertheless shrewd and intensely loyal. When she decided to do something, then she followed it through, no matter what. She was destroyed as much by the Picasso industry as by Picasso, and in a elegant irony, she found that when the artist died, she was like the mistletoe upon a tree that has been cut down. Without the sustenance of that peculiar relationship, she withered and died.

I have taken one definite liberty with the facts – as known – of her life in that my Jacqueline uses a shotgun rather than a pistol to end her torment.

~

Blackness.

In the darkness we can hear the wind . Exterior shutters on the windows are banging and rattling. Just as JACQUELINE turns on the light, a door bangs in the distance. She starts, her head darting round in that direction. Then she relaxes.

The thrum of rain starts to beat a tattoo on the roofs and the windows. It will rise and decrease in intensity, occasionally becoming torrential.

She is now standing mid stage. Behind her a curtain on which are painted – in monochrome – huge arched windows protected by grillwork shutters. The effect is as of a movie in black and white.

She is slight of figure, but thickening around the waist and she is wearing what at first seems to be an ample dress but is really a peignoir, decorated with large white daisies. Her hair is dishevelled as she has just got out of bed, donned slippers etc., and come straight here without so much as combing her hair. Initially she is somewhat 'distraite', finding it difficult to establish eye contact and tending to close in on herself.

She eyes us warily, as if speaking only under sufferance.

JACQUELINE: When I was a child, learning my catechism, they taught me that life was a vale of tears.
One must bear everything with fortitude: learn to be a good wife, a good mother.
I did. I was... a good wife... to Pablo.
They did not tell me that the next life was simply repetition, repetition, repetition...
(*She looks around with a tolerant, perhaps resigned, yet amused wonderment.*)

Every morning, before he wakes up – and he rarely wakes up before eleven, rarely goes to bed before dawn breaks – every morning I come to sit in whichever studio he is working... the whole house is his studio... dozens of rooms... (*Goes to the white rocking-chair plumped with cushions.*) and I sit in his white rocking-chair, feeling myself meld into the cushions that have plumped to his shape, feeling my arms become his as they slide along the arm-rests, feeling my hands become his as if his brushes were my brushes in his hands which are mine, feeling his eyes survey the tiny mountains of crushed paint-tubes scattered along the floor, feeling my uterine muscles twitch, tense and push as the thick membranes of impasto slide and swirl and stain the canvas.

(*Walking towards a large easel, opened but with just an empty frame upon it. There are two studio lights fixed to the top of it, for night-time work.*)

(*With quiet satisfaction.*) There! There! There is our
canvas, the canvas of our dreams.
Memories, hallucinations, this world, our world, the
studio, me, me, me, me as whatever he wanted me to be –
Look! Canvases stacked, back to back, their birthdays
written on the reverse.
(*Taking a comb from her pocket and combing her hair.*) Ceramics,
lithographs, engravings, drawings, sculpture in plaster,
sheet-metal, bronze, silver... linocuts. This man, even at
ninety-two, kept on producing paintings, sculptures,
prints, my children, our babies...

Look at the studio tables: pencils, crayons, varnishes, old
brushes, new brushes, old paints, new paints, the lightbulb
without a shade, the wax-apple candle, the small stack of
faded paintboxes hoarded from his days at the Bateau
Lavoir. A note in his own hand tells me that they were
bought in 1905 with money from Gertrude Stein 'for the
first picture she got from me'.

(*She leans forward and stares at the 'painting' on the easel.*)
He sleeps, gathering his energies and inside his head,
his brushes erect, he scores on the canvas. While he
sleeps, I complete. I wait and watch and protect,
urging my babies into the harsh world. I lavish my
eyes upon them, give them tenderness and love so
that when their father comes they are ready to
receive him...
(*A particularly fierce wind-whipped torrent of rain. We hear rivulets
of it running down the gutters. She shivers and wraps her peignoir
tightly around her.*)

When I was living in Haute Volta – they call it Burkina
Faso now – it was like this: violent storms with the rains
lasting from June to October.
Doesn't happen too often in the Midi!

(*She suddenly twists her body, head directly facing the audience,
and speaks with urgent authority:*)

Vauvenarges. Château. Cézanne country. He thought he'd
bottled the essence not only of the painter's landscapes but
of Cézanne himself. Pointed to a window and told me. 'All
I have to do is put a frame around it and sign it!' Eating
Cézanne for breakfast, lunch and dinner.
I hated the place.
Fortunately, he soon had indigestion.
(*Relaxing and going back to the rocking chair.*)

I married a Monsieur Hutin, a colonial civil servant,
and we lived at Ouagadougou.
On the map, it's in the centre of Haute Volta.
Like the map it's flat. Flat dirty streets lined with garbage
and flat hungry goats.
So hot that your clothes stick to your back and your legs
and your arms. So dusty that every clammy inch of you
is stained a dusky red.
In daytime the vultures shamble in the sky, searching
for scraps.
At night inky streaks, flutter and flit.
Catherine was born.

I was always tired. I hated the food: bean and banana
fritters, yam *frites*. And he wanted more children and it
was so oppressively hot and clammy and sticky with your
skin like a suction pad against his. When I had the first
operation they told me that it was unlikely I could have
any more children; but he wanted to stay, and he wanted
children and he wanted... just wanted... so, one day, I told
him I was leaving and I did, telling him he could have a
divorce anytime *he* wanted.
It didn't take him long.
And I took Catherine.

(*She stands up and stares at the picture frame on the easel.*)
(*We hear what she hears in her head. It is Maurice Chevalier singing*
You've Got That Thing. The wind and the rain are recessed. Memories
of her dancing classes come back to her and she sways and moves to the
music, and then sings along with the following verse:)

Your fetching physique is hardly unique
You're mentally not too hot
You'll never win Laurels because of your morals
But I'll tell you what you've got...
You've got that thing... etc.

(*She stops with a smile upon her face, her arms wrapped around her shoulders: a private moment. The wind and the rain creep back. Then she takes a little moisturiser from a bottle in her pocket and rubs it sensuously into her skin and applies lipstick during the following:*)
(*Points.*) A part of me.
Every morning I come and watch a part of me.
I open the shutters, the windows, let the children breathe.
This is my time. Not Picasso's time. My time.

I can hear him. Wherever he is. Twenty-two rooms.
Three floors.
His first cough of the morning. The irritable shambling of sheets.
La France will be making breakfast which I will take in.

If he's in a bad mood the rolling thunder of the big easel on castors spurts and splutters as he shoves it irritably.
I can hear him, pacing, picking up things, dropping them, scuffing the ceramics, rifling through art books.
(*The half curtain begins to slowly rise. Equally slowly the rain and wind die away to be replaced by the warm light of a Cannes summer.*)
But when the curtain rises, if the throes of birthing are eating at his guts, he chews the pain blissfully, silently, the only sound the faint scratching of brush on canvas; or on a summer's day the cicadas humming a harmony on the ethic of work.

(*We become aware of another smaller easel behind the curtain. During the following JACQUELINE is assembling her suicide machine: rigging a shotgun to the easel, so that it points outwards, horizontally and firmly.*)
Perhaps you think I am stupid? I should have stayed with my husband in Africa?
Perhaps. But I knew I was missing something.

I knew that if I stayed in that dreary, dreary colony,
I would simply chafe. So few women to talk to. So little
to do.
So I knew little of art or books or music.
But was I going to find them amidst cholera, yellow
fever or malaria?

I decided to return to the Midi: but far from parental
disapproval. So I took a tiny house at Golfe-Juan, looked
around, and on the beach I met Hugvette who was the
daughter-in-law of the Madame Ramié who ran a pottery
in Vallauris.

(*With a quiet but firm inner intensity.*)
First one decides what is wanted. Then one decides how
to get it.
The one thing my papa always told me – he thought
I wasn't very bright – was that persistence always pays
off. If you set your mind to do something, and you have
the willpower, then you will bend people to your will...
eventually.
Be nice to people he told me. Be patient, charming; do as
they bid you.
Make yourself indispensable.
I suppose he thought he had succeeded when I married
Monsieur Hutin.
And in a way he had.
But I knew I could do better.

I was agreeable to Hugvette so it was natural that
I should be introduced to Madame Ramié, and soon
I was working, part time, in the retail shop in Rue
d'Antibes.
I was agreeable to the customers.
I had reasonable English and Spanish and naturally I was
available whenever I was asked, for whatever I was asked.
One day I met Monsieur Picasso, so naturally I spoke to
him in Spanish.

His eyes lit like candles and he almost gabbled in pleasure, complimenting me on my figure, my eyes, my dress sense and my Spanish; so naturally I complimented him, telling him how youthful he looked and how absolutely utterly amazing were his decorations on the ceramics and how ever so many people were asking for them and talking about them and saying how incredibly wonderful they were.

So he kept coming back to see me.

Naturally.

Madame Ramié was most pleased.

There were a few problems with Monsieur Picasso's home-life.

That awful woman Françoise.

He was seeing other women. Of course whatever Monsieur Picasso wanted was fine by Madame Ramié but wouldn't it be a pity if he decided to move away from Vallauris? Such a loss to the town.

And he does seem to like you Jacqueline so we must work together Jacqueline, you and I, to ensure that Monsieur Picasso gets what Monsieur Picasso wants.

So sometimes I would drive down to La Galloise, Picasso's house, with boxes of ceramics for him to paint.

I was very nice to Françoise and when I knew she wasn't there I would call in to ask Monsieur if there was any way I could help him.

She left him in September 1953.

I was in the right place and at the right time but I knew that it was *not* going to be easy. Monsieur Picasso was beseiged once it was known that Françoise had left.

So many hangers-on.

He started haunting night-clubs, all along the Côte d'Azur, always with a retinue of useless, self-serving, supposed friends. Once three girls came up to him for his autograph so he tells them to dress their prettiest,

go to the hairdresser's, and then invites them for dinner
that night. Shameless hussies!
What kind of behaviour is that for a man of over
seventy!

Around the beginning of December I intercepted a
telegram from Françoise saying that she was coming for
Christmas with the children. So I gave it to Madame
Ramié who met Françoise at the station and persuaded
her to return home, leaving the children.
Before long I was looking at that woman's dresses, in
Pablo's bedroom.
'Why don't you try them on?' he said... standing there...
waiting... so I did... but she was slenderer than me.
Pablo came over and tried to do up the hooks. He spent
a long time, opening up and elongating them.
Then he helped me undress and suggested I try another.
He liked touching me. I knew he was wondering how far
could he go, so I just bowed my head, kept my eyes
looking down and waited.
I moaned a little, every now and then.
I think men like that.

It's really quite boring – so much nicer just to be curled
up in bed, warm, comfortable, relaxed, just touching – but
men need other things so it is necessary to give them what
they want... little by little... to steer them in the direction
you want them to go.

If I was patient, agreeable, indispensable, I could be living
with this man.
I would not be a nobody. People would have to pay
attention to me.
I could exist in his paintings... forever! I could be
comfortable, all the time.
I need never worry.
But I wasn't stupid. I could see that everyone wanted
something. Most gave nothing in return. I could see

that this man was all-powerful.
If I was to have any power myself, it would take a long
time to obtain it and I would have to be very, very
careful; very, very clever; very, very much more
intelligent than people thought I was.
So, naturally, I was!

I made it my business to be always there, available,
for whatever he wanted. The important thing was to
make him think that I had to be wooed; that I did
what was necessary for the sake of his art. So he
sketched me fully clothed, lying on the chaise longue.
Then in shorts. Then with my top rolled up. Then
with nothing on underneath my rolled-up top. I let
him rouge my nipples erect. Then I let him open my
legs with his pencil... let him widen each crevice
and crack, let him stipple every black curly hair as
he mapped his erections in the infinite compass of
my groans.

It was easy. I thought of what I would make for dinner,
what clothes I would have to buy and what I could afford,
and I let him play with his imagination.
But would it be enough?
How many others had opened simply in hope of a
quick sketch?

(*With pride.*) I knew what to do with a man like this.
Was he hungry. No?
Then I would wait.
Did he need water? Canvases from the shop in the town?
Phonecalls to be made?
A man like this does not want to be bothered with the
mundane.
He does not wish to waste his time in petty trifles.
I checked the times his medicines needed to be taken.
What were his favourite *tizanes*. And I could drive,
interpret for him if English or American dealers and

critics should come; speak to his Spanish friends. If he
wanted rid of someone, he could speak to me in Spanish
with a smile and I would find an excuse to tell his friends
to go – for a man like Pablo never wants to be in the
wrong; never wants to be seen as unfriendly.

And if I know little about art at this point in my life,
I know the world thinks that this is a great man; and that
a man needs to be told, regularly, that he *is* great, and
that if I tell him that each new work is a masterpiece
then he will want to produce more masterpieces because
we all want to be loved, don't we?

(*She smiles to herself, takes off her peignoir, and starts to dress.
Fly in a cut-out of one of the early portraits of Jacqueline. She stares
at it.*)

June the second and third, 1954. We knew we were in
with a chance.

When Madame Ramié saw them she almost crowed with
delight: three full-scale portraits. Of me. Me.

Me. Memememememe!

(*With an edge.*) For two years I had known him, waited on
him, been available to him and not once had he painted me.
He meets that English woman, that prissy blonde who
thinks she is so sophisticated and cool, (*Bitterly.*) and
inside a month he makes forty – forty! – drawings and
paintings of the hussy: forty unsuccessful attempts to get
inside her knickers.

And that... that trollope Laporte, doesn't she turn up all
over the place, sliding through his work like quicksilver.
What did he see in either of them?

Breasts no bigger than a pair of dried figs. Figures like
knitting needles: straight up and straight down.

You can see both of them in my portraits. Laporte's
elongated neck. The English woman's steely
sophistication.

(*Tenaciously.*) But it's me that he painted: this nose,

this eye, this mouth. Me.
I was entering him and elements of me were creaming
out onto canvas.

And then what does the bastard go and do? When
they honour him by doing the impossible – having a
bullfight at Vallauris in his honour when such a thing
is banned by the government – he asks Françoise to
perform the opening ceremony on horseback.
Françoise! That bitch!
Not me. Françoise!
Who does the wee shite think he is?
I went straight to Madame Ramié: 'This is intolerable'.
She agreed. Arranged for me to take horse-riding lessons.
But I kept falling off.

And then, before the ceremony, when Françoise comes to
La Galloise, and naturally I'm hiding in the adjoining
room, don't I hear the bastard telling her that the only
right and proper thing would be for her and the children
to come and live with him again!

So I have to swallow my pride and remember that he is
seventy this man and that all men are ruled by their cocks
and that this can be turned to advantage.
I have to remember that most of these women do not
want to spend their time doing the real work of waiting
and watching and organising and looking after him
properly. Didn't all of his trousers have holes in the
pockets because he kept stuffing them with whatever
rubbish he found along the beach or the street? Wasn't
it me who made sure that his pockets were sewn, that he
bought new trousers, that his shirts were clean and
pressed, that he ate properly?
Oh there was so much that I wanted to do – but he was
very peremptory this man.
If I wanted to dust he could howl into a rage or if I
tried to throw out some of the clutter he could explode

into violence: was I trying to ruin his life, to deprive
him of his inspiration? Wasn't I just a stupid,
thick-headed woman, only good for fucking or cleaning?
Women were either goddesses or doormats and I was a
doormat and
I had better not forget it!

So I knew what I had to do and I dressed prettily and
I went to the bullfight and I sat beside Monsieur Picasso
and I met Cocteau who sat on Monsieur Picasso's other
side and I was very very nice to Cocteau who was
flattered and I smiled and I watched that bitch Françoise
strut around on her prancing horse, and I determined
that I was going to win.
No matter what he said, or did, I was going to be beside
him. (*Beat.*)

He treated me like a servant. Do this, do that, fetch my
pills, open your legs, fuck off, bend over, get this, get
that, where's my *tizane*?; are you stupid, woman?, fetch
my pills!
All this in front of friends or acquaintances or strangers,
and me having brought him his pills, not ten minutes
beforehand.

So now he's going down to Perpignan to the aristocratic
Lazermes, and I can tell you, I'm going too, and I do.
Everywhere he goes, I go, but I'm having to stay in a
hotel because he won't let me stay at the Lazermes even
though his entire party is there, but I can't keep track of
him with my daughter around my neck so I put her out
to board in the mountains.

(*With an edge of triumph.*) And now his illegitimate
daughter Maya has left the Lazermes so he has no excuse
and I move into her bed and doesn't he move in too,
and I am very very attentive to Monsieur and Madame
Lazerme and I admire everything in the house and
compliment them on the food and their servants and their

impeccable taste and if I can be of use, if they should need
to be driven anywhere, haven't I my car?
And then doesn't the bastard tell me that Françoise is
coming next week so naturally she'll sleep with him while
she's there and I can move out until she's gone so I tell
him, oh no I won't and oh no she won't!
And he throws a temper tantrum, screaming at me that
I'll fucking do whatever he fucking well wants or I can
fucking well leave, and we can be heard all over the
house so I told him to fuck off and stormed out of the
house and drove off!

Which was stupid.

I phoned at lunchtime from Norbonne but he wouldn't
even come to the phone.
I waited for half an hour then phoned again. Madame
Lazerme answered.
I told her I would kill myself if he didn't come to the
phone. After a while he did.
I told him I was wrong and he was right and that I loved
him and that he had to give me another chance otherwise
I would kill myself.
'Suit yourself' he said and put the phone down.

That evening I drove back and asked for Madame
Lazerme.
'He told me to suit myself Madame so I'm back.'
What else could she do but give me my room again?
Picasso didn't look too pleased to see me.
I rushed up to him and kissed his hands, called him
my Lord and Master; told him that I would do anything
for him.
And I did.

I trailed after him.
Wherever he went I made him look good.
I was devoted.

And I knew I would have allies.

Wasn't he spending an awful amount of time in
Perpignan? Weren't ever so many people trying to get
him to stay there?

So suddenly all of his other friends, from Paris and
Vallauris especially, were coming to see him and weren't
the Pignons, the Ramiés, the Leiris's all trying to enlist my
help to make sure that Picasso returned to Vallauris?

So weren't they all telling him how lucky he was to have a
young attractive woman to help him, a young woman who
loved him, who doted on him, who would do anything for
him, a young woman who was a good cook, a good
housekeeper, a good organiser, who would look after him
and keep him satisfied in every respect; and wasn't he a
wag to be able to attract a woman like that, a woman who
was over forty years younger than him! And didn't she
make it abundantly clear to everyone that he was the Lord
and Master!

And no matter what he said to me, no matter how
much he cursed me or cut me dead or slighted me,
I would still be there, kissing his hands, telling
everyone how wonderful he was, and when we went to
bed at night I would give him whatever he wanted, let
him open my legs and eat me as his hors d'oeuvre, let
him thrust into me and fire off, and I would suck him
till he sighed to sleep.

And it worked.

And didn't I enjoy the look of surprize on the faces of
Monsieur et Madame Lazerme when Picasso decided to
go back to Vallauris – with me!

We would go straight to Paris where I would move in
with him!

Naturally I went through La Galloise with a very fine
tooth-comb.

(*Deadpan.*) All of Françoise's dresses I gave to the local
charities.

Anything else that was of use I had crated.

If one is going to organise a campaign, one needs to be meticulous and to think ahead.

Paris was a breathing space. The master's friends, acquaintances, leeches, hangers-on arrived like flies to a flypaper. I watched from the shadows. If I was to be of use to this man, I needed to learn: who was useful to him, who was not?; who was a wastrel, who was not?; who was a threat, who was not? I needed to know about art, about Picasso's art, and as there were hundreds of books about art and hundreds more about Picasso, I started to read them.

I listened: to every critic, every poet, every journalist, every curator.

I learnt the different periods and their dates: Blue period, Rose period, Cubist period... I learnt the names of all his friends, of all the artists, and which ones he liked, which ones were a threat to him, which ones he couldn't stand.

I learnt the technicalities of printmaking by talking to the technicians and all the time I listened to Pablo because I could learn about his world, about his past, about him.

(*Abruptly she turns to the audience and speaks with a blunt intensity.*)

November, 1954. Matisse dies.

'The only real threat', said Pablo. 'Now I can steal!'

December. Delacroix. *The Women of Algiers.*

The Louvre version.

That's you, he said, pointing to the woman who crouches in the right hand corner.

And it was. He ate Matisse and he gorged on Delacroix and he painted me as all the things that Laporte and the English woman weren't: sensuous, sensual, ripely plump – an odalisque. Hadn't I come to him from Africa? Wasn't I now a part of his harem?

– And wasn't I going to make sure that I was the only one in his harem?

One of these days, this man was going to marry me, whether he wanted to or not!

179

Time to go back to Vallauris. I had need of support.
Time to build up *my* retinue.
Now people were beginning to need me. I was
the conduit.
Françoise owned La Galloise so I instructed Madame
Ramié to find a proper house, as befitting the station
of the most famous painter in the world and so within
a month we were moving into La Californie, once
owned by the Moët family. Of champagne fame! Didn't
it look oriental – as if The Women of Algiers had been
living there!
And me, Jacqueline Hutin, née Roque, ex housewife, ex
part-time salesgirl, wasn't I now about to live in a villa
in Cannes with Monsieur Pablo Picasso, the most famous
artist in the world!

(*Trying unsuccessfully not to let her very real pleasure show
through.*)
Cannes! The Riviera proper! Casinos, palm trees, fields
of violets, a funicular railway! And of course we were on
the most exclusive part called La Californie, high up on
the slope with magnificent views over the bay of Cannes
– not to mention a gatekeeper's lodge at the bottom of
the driveway.
I gave the gatekeeper and his wife their instructions. No
entry to anyone unless I gave specific instructions; or The
Master did.
Oh there was such magnificent furniture in the house.
Even white grand pianos!
But Picasso got rid of almost everything, even the deep-pile
carpets and the tapestried curtains: the entire house became
his studio.

'Who needs that junk?' he said, bringing in his own junk
by the lorryload.
Crates piled up under the marble staircase, spilled out into
the entrance hall and like vigourous vines, crept along the
corridors and into any available room.

A sofa covered with a raggedy pearl-grey cover replaced
the white leather one he threw out; broken, scratched and
bursting furniture came from *all* his previous homes: Rue
Ravignan, La Boétie, Boisgeloup, Grands-Augustins.
Stacks of tiles took root, bullfight posters, ceramics,
canvases, coffeepots, wierd wooden sculptures from the
Congo or wherever that some witchdoctor must have
used; dozens of easels, endless stacks of books, photos,
magazines, newspapers, letters, ornaments, unopened
presents, clothes, towers of cigarette packets, lamps, toys,
bronzes, paintings stuck up on any available nail,
bulging portfolios, hundreds of painting brushes, the tide
advancing across the floors, rising over tables, chairs,
settees, plant pots, fireplaces.
And nothing could be taken away from where it was,
or tidied. Specific rooms were requisitioned: a drawing
room for storing canvases, stacked back to back;
a kitchen as engraving studio; a bathroom for
lithography.

He hated change, this man. Odd. Does not every book,
every critic say that in his work he changes all the
time? But in life this man wanted things to be as they
always were.
He wrapped himself with mementos, hated to throw
anything away, loved photographs – and soon I realized
that he made the world around him and then painted it
into *his* world, so that if I were always present then I too
would be a part of this world, and not just when he
wanted to do a portrait.
If he always used what was there, then it followed that it
was necessary to *be* there.
So I didn't have the education of a Françoise or a Dora,
but they didn't manage what I did!
He painted me, me, more than he painted any of his
other women!

Jacqueline as Mater Dolorosa, as odalisque, Jacqueline

in a Spanish shawl, in Turkish garb, Jacqueline in a
Black Scarf, with the cat, with the dog, Jacqueline in
Delacroix, Velásquez, Manet, Rembrandt, Jacqueline
naked, nude, standing, sitting, with legs crossed,
uncrossed, Jacqueline in paintings, drawings,
watercolours, lithographs, engravings, etchings,
linocuts, on sculptures in bronze, steel, wood, plaster,
ceramic, Jacqueline on tiles, a world of Jacquelines,
Jacqueline peering out of book after book, not
to mention Jacqueline photographed by Picasso,
photographed by famous people like Brassai and
Duncan, photographed by the press. And of course the
world now needed me to get to Picasso so they started
to be very, very nice to me but I remembered all of
those who were not so nice to me in the early days...
(*a long beat.*) Papa was right: everything comes to the
person who waits...

I observed his routines and I built my routines around
them. Certain things he was going to accept. He could
dress as he wished but he was going to have clean
clothes, fashionable clothes, clothes made by a proper
tailor and properly washed and pressed and without
holes. I needed to organise properly so there was a
lady from ten until four, and another from four until
ten. I insisted upon that.
The gatekeeper's husband would be the gardener. And
I wanted fresh vegetables.
Picasso may not like things moved but that did not mean
that they could not be dusted.
I gave strict instructions: dusting between, around,
and of each and every object but nothing to be moved
– ever.

Food would be served at regular times. If he did not want it,
then additional meals would be made when he did want. The
shutters would be closed and opened at regular times,
likewise the windows to ensure that every room was aired.

He was going to see a doctor and a dentist at regular
intervals.
He was going to take his homeopathic drops, and the
lineament for his leg muscles at regular intervals.
He was going to eat his carrot and pea soup to soothe
the ulcer in his stomach.
He was going to become dependent on me.

It did not occur to me that I was going to become
completely dependent on him...

Fair is fair. I wanted to be with this man. Therefore he had
a right to do with me as he wished. He liked animals:
dogs, cats, parrots, pigeons, doves, goats. Was sentimental
about them – not a countryman.
Esmeralda the goat lived on the second floor in a wooden
crate. She would lick his hands and climb up onto his lap.
She stank.
In the mornings she left a trail of small round droppings
along the landings.
The dogs chewed them like sweets.
I had to wash her regularly in rosewater.
In one of the balconies he built a pigeon loft out of packing
cases. So doves and pigeons would fly into the rooms and
spread their liquid droppings all over the sheets and the
parquet floors.
I insisted on a washing machine.
He was very proud of it. Whenever visitors came we would
take them to the kitchen and even if there was no washing
to be done we would put clean napkins or tableclothes into
the wash and watch it spin and spin. He would laugh and
tell us how his mother would have been terrified at such a
machine but wasn't it a marvel. Such energy! A spinning
white world like a harnessed hurricane!

And then there were the grand days. No visitors. Pablo
working happily, alone on the ground floor. A soft
silence. I would perhaps sit in my 'salon' on the second

floor, the windows open to the scented sunshine of eucalyptus, mimosa and pine; the bay of Cannes gleaming beneath the thick blue of the sky, perhaps dotted with the American fleet; the isles of Lérins with the *son et lumière* floating across the windless bay; the only other sounds the buzz of a bumble bee as it thwacked into a canvas, stunned itself, and was then carried by Pablo to a branch in the garden... or the rustling whirr of pigeon's wings as they nestled and cooed on the balcony.

I might sit on the steps outside a studio window, shaded by the crowns of high palms, breathing in the sea air, and rest my gaze on the oleander, the honeysuckle or the medlars. Jan, and all of the other dogs, would be farting and slavering in the afternoon sun, pushing a pebble along the drive in an effort to get you to play. Esmeralda, the goat, would be tethered to Pablo's bronze goat, hoping that he would come and take her for a walk. The woman with the orange – Pablo called her the iron mistress – would be standing guard beside the door. Jan, and all of the other dogs, used to pee on it and all of the other bronzes. Picasso said it helped the patination and if we had a dinner party he would lead the men out at night, telling them they'd never find another *pissoir* like it!

I might curl up on the sofa, or sit behind him on the floor of a studio, or watch him as he sat in his rocking chair, flicking ash into the miniature tyres of an ashtray, eyes lancing into his work, thinking, analysing, waiting for the moment.

If things went wrong and the work wouldn't come, then everything was rotten, spoiled, and he would snap and snarl and rant and demand to know what you had done with his stick of chalk which was under the book he was looking at – on the table. He would complain bitterly that the visitor he hadn't wanted to see was deliberately sent away by me; that I was starving him of affection,

company and food; that he didn't get enough sex; that
the rain was my fault, the sun was my fault, the visit of
one of his children had been arranged by me to torment
him; couldn't I see that it was imperative that he not
be bothered?

So I bowed my head and I let him rant until he had
nothing left to say, and then I would gently take him by
the arm, fetch him a bowl of icecream – he loved
icecream – or a stick of ginger, and I would massage
his shoulders, and kiss his hands and tell him that he
owed it to the world to continue the exercise of his
amazing gifts.

Sometimes he would just walk to another room, banging
the door as he left, but often he would quieten down, sit
in his rocking chair and I would fetch him a sketchbook
and a splay of pencils and quietly sit in the corner,
reading a book on a man called Picasso.

And there were advantages. Everyone wanted to see him.
I met novelists and poets, actors and filmstars, politicians
and heads of state. One day Gary Cooper phoned and I
persuaded Pablo to see him.

(*Breathlessly.*) Gary Cooper – wasn't he gorgeous and
magnificent and oh so upright and handsome in *High
Noon*!

And I met Gary Cooper, really, the actual Gary Cooper,
wearing his cowboy hat and his cowboy boots and
bringing a cowboy's revolver for Pablo. He didn't speak
French so I was the only one who could talk to him, and
he kissed my hand and then he kissed me on both
cheeks, and he put the gun in his hand and he twirled it
round and round, just like a cowboy in the films and so
Pablo took us all to dinner in one of his favourite
restaurants and didn't all of the diners and all of the
waitresses and the waiters come up and ask for Gary
Cooper's autograph and poor Pablo was ignored!

Just imagine: being married to Gary Cooper!!

(We hear the opening verse of the song from High Noon, <u>Do Not Forsake Me ,Oh My Darling</u>.)
(Her eyes burn with pleasure and she sways sensually to the rhythm, her arms crossed over her breasts as if she were dancing with him. As the song fades, she seems to become old before us: old, dried-up, tired. Abruptly she snaps out of it.)

On March the second, 1961, I did it! Officially.
We returned from Vallauris and poured champagne for our staff.
I was now Mrs Pablo Picasso.
I knew what he wanted, so I gave it to him, regularly.
Within three months we had moved to a new home, a luxurious villa in Mougins which was in my name. I had an Intercom system installed and an electronically-controlled gate. Guard dogs roamed in the grounds at night. This was now my world too.
He was an old man. He needed protecting: from the autograph hunters and dealers, from his friends, from his illegitimate children, from himself.
And he began a winter blossoming!
1962: seventy-three Jacquelines.
1973: a hundred and sixty-two Jacquelines!

We lived on a terraced hillside with a long avenue of ancient olive trees, iron-grey and laden with olives. Behind, a screen of cypresses. In front, in the distance, the tiled ochre roofs of Mougins and beyond that, the glittering greens and blues of the bay of Cannes.
In the bedroom, my clothes, my lipstick, my moisturiser would now stay...

As always, papa was right. If you haven't the power, the money, the force of personality to get your way immediately, then do it little by little. So I did.
Naturally. This was a warm, comfortable, well-furnished house.
Picasso did as Picasso always did, Pablo got whatever

Pablo wanted but his world was changing. He was
becoming, even for Pablo... old.
Death was now a presence.

(*She snaps round urgently, facing us in half profile. Rembrandt's*
The Night Watch is projected in all its vastness onto the back wall.
Then – snap, snap, snap – a series of Rembrandt's self-portraits,
starting with Rembrandt as a young man and ending with the
pitiless dissection of Rembrandt as an old man.)
(*This slide remains.*)

Rembrandt. *The Night Watch.* The self-portraits.
Projecting the slides onto the wall so that he could
enter that world.
Eating Rembrandt.
Watching Rembrandt watch himself as the years
rippled towards the grim reaper...

Was it his fault that he was becoming old, deaf,
shortsighted?
He was my Pablo and it was my job to ease the pain.
He called me *maman* and he loved me to bathe him in
the bath, to scrub his back and soap his shoulders and
pat his bottom dry.
In his rocking chair, if he wanted to draw, I would cover
his legs with a thick wool blanket, and bring him hot soup
and *tizanes*, read him his letters as he lay in bed, and at
night, I would stroke his forehead, and kiss him on the
neck and push my body into his so that he would keep
warm, and quietly rock him to sleep, always amazed that
these broad shoulders and wrinkled arms would be rising
in the morning to take the brush or the burin and birth
my babies into the light of day...
And he was grateful, so grateful... and when it would
start, he would come shouting to the studio door,
yelling 'Jacqueline, Jacqueline, they're coming!
They're coming!'

Françoise published that fucking pile of lies, Pablo had
prostate problems and could no longer perform, and

those bitches and bastards of his children were now litigating. What did they think they were doing these, these... these shites?

They were mauling at his mind, hacking at *him*; he was eating all of their shite and disgorging it in his work. He was hating his body, my body, any body, taking it out on me as a blubber of flesh: flesh sloughing and sliding, mashing and merging; flesh as a sticky, dribbly miasma of leering, screwing, fucking, shitting, deformed slop, swimming with disappearing clitorises, and floppy penises and bloated repulsive faces and vulvas and me, me, me as a live carcass, squatting and pissing on the floor –

(*A long ululating scream of agony.*) – Me!

(*Almost beside herself.*) And then he would work on the copper, the voyeur, lusting after the svelte slut that his fingers would score on the plate, with her pert, firm, nipple-eyed breasts and her sloe eyes and her long slim legs and her long slim fingernails sliding and spreading her succulent vulva lips until they gaped as wide as the fucking french windows of his studio – and there he was, scored into the plate, artistus erectus, his eyes, ravishing, rutting, raping – while... all the while, in his lap, underneath the plate, his limp prick stubbornly refused to quicken.

(*She is sucking in great mouthfuls of air, like a patient in shock who is trying to stop herself from fainting. All of her willpower, her ability to shape herself into a willed construction – comes into play.*)

I made myself see what was happening. He was not to blame. They were.

He was castrated and he needed relief. He needed me to cosset him, gentle him...

He needed me to stop the nasty outside world ripping into him...

He needed me to gently guide him to let our proper children emerge into the waiting world.

Monsieur Rance, our local doctor, came every day.
No excitement. He must not be excited in any way.
Whatever Picasso wanted...
He never saw obstacles, did Pablo...
Hadn't he been in hospital last year? Pulmonary
congestion. Weak heart.

(*She smiles.*) He was in his beige pyjamas and I knew that
something was wrong.
So I phoned Doctor Bernard in Paris who drove straight
for a plane.
When he arrived in the morning, I relaxed, for the good
doctor was a specialist and I knew Pablo would be safe.
How could he leave me?
He didn't have the right to leave me...

The fingers of his hands were blue and swollen and he
was gasping for breath.
He mentioned Apollinaire and told the doctor that he
should get married as it was useful. The only sound,
above the rattly gasp, was the rustling of the roses against
the window. And when I turned from the window the
doctor was standing up and I told him, 'My Monseigneur
is safe, and I thank you', and he told me that Pablo was
dead, and I told him that he was mistaken for Pablo was
smiling, and I must take off my dressing-gown and get
into bed to keep him warm; and I lay there, keeping him
warm, for he was my Pablo, and he could not leave me,
and I would not let him leave me, for he did not have the
right to leave me... did he?

And the phone kept on ringing and ringing and ringing
and the house was surrounded by crowds of nasty people,
and I told his children and all those other hangers-on
that no, no, no, no, they were not going to the funeral,
this was *our* funeral...
(*The Rembrandt slide goes out of focus and fades.*)

(*Over the following the lights begin to darken as in a black and white movie.*)

I had to organise.
I covered my Pablo in a black Spanish shawl.
It was raining. Heavily. At five o'clock in the morning the hearse came.
We were going to Vauvenargues: a proper, respectful, quietude.
As we drove through the night, along the mountain route, it began to snow and snow and we had to stop. Eventually a snowplow came and it was necessary to return to the highway and when we arrived at Vauvenargues the gravediggers could not break the ground and so we had to wait until pneumatic drills ripped into the white frozen world, and the birds rose in black clouds above the crystalline white of the branches, and then... it was over.

(*Now the winds begin to freshen and the rain begins to thrum and then become torrential. A sudden, very violent crack as when a tree begins to uproot itself, then falls, crashing into the undergrowth. She blesses herself instinctively. She walks over to her contraption of the shotgun mounted on the small easel. It is getting very dark. As she reaches the easel, the two spotlights mounted on the other easel suddenly blaze on, illuminating her. She is stroking the barrels of the gun.*)

He was my Pablo. The studio was his stage. We had our props, our costumes, our rituals, our lights. I was the bride stripped bare and we made love. He was my master, my monseigneur, my God...

And now the vultures came. And they wanted to scatter his seed, our children, to the four corners of the earth. And they came in their striped suits with their striped tongues and their neat ledgers and every painting, every dress, every knick-knack and pair of shoes and every photograph and every letter and every part of us

they itemised, walking in their shiny shoes and their
soft voices over every part of my house and every sheet
of my writing, and for three years they stayed there,
eating me and eating Pablo; and the other vultures, his
little bastards and bitches, wanted only to get their
claws into my Pablo and scatter him to the four winds
of auction houses and fat cheques; and they scratched
and they scratched and they scratched but I didn't give
in and if they gouged out chunks of my flesh, at least
I managed to preserve a substantial part, and I didn't
disperse it, did I?
I toured Picasso's Picassos to the four corners of the
world, and I set up a shrine to his memory, a museum
for Pablo, where my children could breathe in the
warmth of the world.

Every night, I set a place for him at dinner. But he
never comes.
Sometimes I think I see him, padding across the parquet
floors, his slippers whispering to the evening air. Monsieur
et Madame are ready to receive...
In the next room the parrot is eating noisily, disrespectfully,
cracking husks of grain, like an old man with no teeth and
hard gums.

*We hear what she hears: it is Maurice Chevalier singing You've Got
That Thing. She sways and glides to the music, and joins in, her
voice soaring, on :*

Your fetching physique is hardly unique
You're mentally not too hot
You'll never win Laurels because of your morals
But I'll tell you what you've got
You've got that thing... etc.

(*The music fades as she pirouettes into silence and immobility.*)
Sometimes I dream that he loved me. Perhaps he did.
Sometimes I dream that I always loved him. And
perhaps I did.
And sometimes, when I have the lights off, and just
the candles burning, I can hear the pitter-patter of tiny

painting feet, and my children come rushing around me, staring at me, loving me, beckoning to me from the walls, and I know that I have no right to be separated from them, and that I have done my duty to the best of my ability, and... and... (*Her voice falters.*) ... and I sometimes wonder if Pablo made me become too harsh towards his other children but that is to be uncharitable for I must have been to blame... but I have always done my duty to Pablo and to our children and they need me, and Pablo needs me, naturally... (*Her fingers are caressing the barrels of the gun.*) ... and I, naturally, need them...

She looks around, as if for one last time, smiling at her children, loving them, and then she leans forward and slips her mouth over and into the gun barrel.
Her finger moves towards the trigger.
Lights snap off.
The shot echoes like a thunderclap as the lights snap on and blood splashes violently over the back wall as her body collapses.
As the lights slowly fade the wind howls and judders and shrieks and the rain beats a tattoo on the roof and runs down the guttering in torrents until finally there is only blackness and the howling of the elements.
And then the song from High Noon, Do Not Forsake Me, Oh My Darling, begins to play and it rises above the howling of the elements as if triumphant, and then it begins to fade, leaving only the howling of the wind and the guttering torrents of the rain restlessly seeking the solace of silence...

The End.

Note: The Maurice Chevalier song is licenced by Long Island Music Co., and is available from Tring International Plc.